CREATIVE AGING

Discovering the Unexpected Joys of Later Life Through Personality Type

Nancy Bost Millner

Foreword by Katharine D. Myers

 Davies-Black Publishing
Palo Alto, California

Published by Davies-Black Publishing, a division of CPP, Inc., 3803 East Bayshore Road, Palo Alto, CA 94303; 800-624-1765.

Special discounts on bulk quantities of Davies-Black books are available to corporations, professional associations, and other organizations. For details, contact the Director of Book Marketing and Sales at Davies-Black Publishing; 650-691-9123; fax 650-623-9271.

Permissions credits are listed on p. 188.

Visit the Davies-Black Publishing Web site at www.daviesblack.com.

07 06 05 04 03   10 9 8 7 6 5 4 3 2
Printed in the United States of America

Cover photograph: © Vera Storman/Tony Stone Images

Library of Congress Cataloging-in-Publication Data
Millner, Nancy B.
      Creative aging : discovering the unexpected joys of later life through
   personality type / Nancy Millner ; foreword by Katharine Myers.
            p. cm.
      Includes bibliographical references.
      ISBN 0-89106-111-8
      1. Aging—Psychological aspects.   2. Typology (Psychology)
   3. Jung, C. G. (Carl Gustav), 1875–1961.   I. Title.
   BF724.8.M55   1997
   155.67′1826—dc21   97–33177
                                                                      CIP

FIRST EDITION
First printing 1997

To my husband, B, fellow journeyer,
and
To my parents, whose "coming to age" period was cut short

CONTENTS

FOREWORD

In *Creative Aging: Discovering the Unexpected Joys of Later Life Through Personality Type*, Nancy Bost Millner makes two major contributions to the literature on aging. First, she presents a fresh perspective that will contribute to the quiet revolution that is taking place in our generally negative cultural attitude toward aging. Second, she is the first author, as far as I know, to explore the impact of personality differences as seen through the lens of Carl G. Jung's psychological type on how we approach and handle the "coming to age" years. By sharing the stories of vital and articulate—but quite human—individuals, she not only opens the door to the potential unexpected joys "reserved for the later years," but also suggests some paths toward these gifts.

Out of her rich experience and with her talent for acute observation, sensitive interviewing, and clear, excellent writing, she provides us with a glimpse into the potential rewards of "coming to age with awareness, with grace, and with great care for one's living." She looks at aging with a healthy realism that neither sugarcoats at the one extreme nor conveys a sense of bleak inevitability at the other. She does not hide from the downside of aging—the diminishments and losses, the fear of helplessness, the fact that some of us end our lives bitter, frustrated, complaining, and joyless; nor does she succumb to the false mythology of the "golden years," as reflected in the ever-present pictures of healthy, youthful-appearing, financially secure couples on golf courses, or in articles about the ninety-year-olds climbing Mt. Everest or performing other such amazing feats.

Millner has chosen to concentrate on those who seem to be aging creatively in order to discover what we may learn from them. Speaking through the words of over fifty men and women, primarily in their sixties and seventies, she pulls together the threads of commonality as well as differences according to differences in personality type. By skillfully laying out Jungian ideas and weaving them into the lives of the elders she has interviewed, she provides a grounded way for readers to shape and direct their own development. Through her application of the Jungian process of individuation, the inner development that can take place toward balance and wholeness, she offers a pathway through our elder years that is challenging and rewarding, and that provides a sense of fulfillment and peace.

Nancy Millner speaks of the gifts reserved for the later years. One of these gifts is the freedom and joy that come through the paradox of becoming more truly oneself and at the same time more at one with all those around us. The process of aging can be pleasantly surprising. Most surprising of all are the unexpected joys, satisfactions, and insights that may more than compensate for the inevitable diminishments. With gentle persuasion, Millner invites us to explore with her and to be open to receiving these gifts by listening to those she interviewed, who have spoken wisely about aging. These are the unexpected joys of the later years—joys that can come only after many years of fruitful living.

I will give this book to my elder peers and to my younger friends. Especially I will give it to my children. Not only will it enable them to understand me better, but it will help shape their attitudes about the potential of the coming to age years in a manner that will serve them well.

—Katharine D. Myers

PREFACE

I have written every poem, every novel,
for the same purpose—to find out what
I think, to know where I stand.

—May Sarton, *Journal of a Solitude*

This book is for people like me who want to find out what they think and to know where they stand in relation to the process of aging in our culture and in our time. It is for those of us who want to understand that period of life when the midlife transition has been navigated and we find ourselves in that long stretch before the last transition of letting go and leaving. It is for us who are young and wish to understand our parents and the older people we work with. It is for us in the middle years who want to age creatively. It is for those of us who do not claim to be young—or even middle aged—but who are not yet old. It is for those interested in that period of life that Jane Pretat (1994) calls "coming to age." And it is specifically for those of us who are interested in identifying the potential gifts of this time.

All life stages have gifts to offer, and all stages have the possibility for stagnation as well. I have explored the midlife awakening and the nature of opportunities and dangers of the midlife transition from a general and a typological perspective with Eleanor Corlett in *Navigating Midlife: Using Typology as a Guide*. After completing that book, I found that I wanted to know more about what happened to people who were able to successfully navigate the middle years and learn from their midlife experiences. I wanted to know more about the coming to age period of life and, particularly, about the gifts of this period for myself and my family, my clients, my friends, and my colleagues. I also wanted to invite our society, which seems miserably unprepared for creative aging, to recognize the gifts of this life stage.

A few people have concerned themselves with this period, but to my knowledge, no one has attempted to differentiate individual journeys in this coming to age stage using the personality theory of psychologist C. G. Jung and the tool of the *Myers Briggs Type Indicator®* (MBTI®) personality inventory. You can read this book without type knowledge, but a knowledge of type can help you enrich and deepen your understanding. As always, the great gift of type investigation is the particularity it can bring to the general. Type is not about generalization. It is about similarities, of course, but as Isabel Myers has taught us, it is also about the creative use of differences. Type study using the MBTI asks, for example, how the ESFJ (a four-letter code indicating a combination of preferences on four dimensions of personality) personality is different from, as well as similar to, the INTJ personality. It also realizes that not only are ESFJs different from INTJs, but each ESFJ is different from all other ESFJs and each INTJ is different from all other INTJs.

There are, of course, many similarities in the coming to age period. Most of us who are interested in the study of aging agree that if the process is successful, people may become more complete, have a sense of integrity about their lives, and become better able to embody wisdom and tolerance. But those of us interested in typology, who believe that people are basically different as well as similar, may want to be a bit more specific. We may indeed, believing in the creative use of differences, want to question how ENFJ completeness can progress and how ENFJ wisdom and tolerance look in comparison to how ISTP completeness can progress and how ISTP wisdom and tolerance look. We may want to recognize that similar destinations are reached by different paths.

This information can be of the most practical assistance as we contemplate our own journeys and those of others. To be able to understand something of our own process of coming to age and to view how others whose personality structures are different from our own come to age allows us to legitimize different approaches as well as to appreciate our own approach by seeing how it is both like and unlike others. But as practical and as helpful as this approach may be, it can also be misused. I have only scratched the surface in my work. I offer you what I have learned in the absolute confidence that it is true and helpful, but I have nothing to say that is not open to revision. In my life and in my work I benefit from having models, and I stand ready to toss them out in the presence of any individual situation in which they are not helpful. My suggestion is that you treat the material of this book in a similar manner.

The material I offer you in these pages relies largely on my own life journey, observation from my work over the past thirty years with people exploring their life journeys, and a series of recent intensive interviews. I recognize, as do many people I interviewed for this book, that when looking back, our lives have formed quite beautiful patterns. The pattern of my life, a pattern of personal journey and of acting as journey guide to others, is one I didn't consciously set out to weave, though I surely had some part in the weaving of it. It is a pattern for which I feel enormous gratitude.

In my twenties, thirties, and early forties I worked as a wife, mother, teacher, and counselor—primarily with people pursuing a sense of identity and vocational interests. By my early forties, I had obtained a position in a university that I had always visualized as the one I would like and was, with my husband, preparing to send two sons off to college. Within a period of several years, I had also lost both parents to death, and "just in time" I began to question what my life was about. For the decade of my forties, I concentrated on the midlife transition and in the book *Navigating Midlife,* which I co-authored with Eleanor Corlett, I dared to suggest some "tasks" for people who would move successfully through the middle passage. Some of these tasks will be revisited briefly in this book. In my own case, midlife led to some significant shifts. Perhaps external changes in the form of a geographic move, a career shift, and a rethinking of the whole field of spirituality were most obvious to others. In my late forties, believing that my psychological training had taken me about as far as it could, I entered a program in spiritual direction. This was a good next step, and I quickly came to know that for me the spiritual could not be separated from the psychological. In my fifties, work has centered primarily around people moving through midlife and emerging from that transition into what I am calling the coming to age period. Three years ago I formed a small nonprofit group that is devoted to personal journey work and the building of a community that can embrace that work, particularly for people in the middle and later years. Then, in the last year, in order to better understand this coming to age period, I sought out a group of people, primarily people in their sixties and seventies, for personal one-on-one interviews. The hope is, of course, that they might cast a little light on the next stage of my journey and of yours as well.

The people I selected to interview appear to be living lives marked by vitality, purpose, and intentionality in this stage beyond midlife. They seem to me—and to others—to be living creatively in the circumstances life has given them. They also confirm that they feel their lives are marked by a sense of personal meaning, though certainly not perfection. They make choices with consciousness. They control the parts of life they can, while realizing there are many areas over which they have little control. They have some capacity for generosity, forgiveness, and ambiguity. They are not simply bound by the mandates of their bodies or environments. They have met some of their personal demons and can call them by name. These selected people have navigated the midlife transition and, to a large extent, adjusted to the changes it required. They are not yet, for the most part, what we would call old. They share many commonalities. Most of them have experienced loss and know something of tears as well as laughter. They have often found that death has a personal face—through the loss of parents, mates, jobs, relationships, or friends, or through some threatening illness of their own. Many have watched children leave home and have experienced the shifting of living and working patterns. Almost all have come to recognize the changes their bodies have announced, and many have recognized that their souls, as well as their bodies, are demanding attention.

This period presents a very different feel from that of the midlife passage. There is a sense of less disruption than during the period of midlife transition. These people coming to age do not experience the urgency of midlife transition questions and the tension of pulls in so many directions. They often find that their lives form a meaningful pattern and that they have a bit more space. They have frequently come to terms, at least to some extent, with limitations and diminishments and have made some peace with the idea of personal death, if not with the process of dying itself.

While writing this book, I interviewed more than fifty people, some of whom you will meet here, and all of whom I learned from. These people (whose names have been changed) range in age from fifty-eight to ninety-four, but are primarily in their sixties and seventies. They are living lives that they feel allow them some opportunity to be authentically who they are and to have some sense of comfort in their universes. These people are not necessarily well known, although others who know them usually recognize them as exceptional individuals. They are male and female, but more are female than male. They are primarily Caucasian but occasionally include a person of African American or mixed ancestry. Most are Christian, at least nominally. Several are Quaker, many of whom also consider themselves Christian, and others are Jewish, Universalist Unitarian, humanist, existentialist, or agnostic. Most have an interest in spiritual issues, sometimes in a traditional religious sense, and often in a very personal and nonconventional sense. A few recognize no such interest. They represent all sixteen type codes. They live in different parts of the United States. They are from differing educational and economic levels, although most are well educated and few would be called either poor or affluent. For all of this attempt to hear different voices, these people are neither adequate in number nor adequately representative of a "typical" population to ever justify any kind of generalization.

All of the people I talked to and most of the people I have worked with over the years have been well-functioning people who live with some awareness and have a great deal to offer others. None of them, however, would say that he or she has arrived at any sense of perfection or that he or she does not still struggle from time to time. These people do not represent what has been called the modern maturity myth, those "slim, blond, smiling couples" who often grace the marketing brochures for senior citizen cruises and retirement villages announcing how getting older should be. Neither are they "creative" people in the limited sense of artist, writer, and musician, although they all live creatively. Nor can they be considered "wise old women/men" waiting to impart their sage and detached advice to young seekers. Often, and usually with a sense of humor, they wonder if anyone wants—or even should want—their advice. One thing they have in common is that they have all lived fully and are all open to reflecting on and learning from their decades of life experience as well as sharing it with others.

About a decade ago, I wrote a dissertation, and later a book, dealing with the dynamics of midlife transition. Both were in large part undertaken to find out what I thought and to know where I stood in regard to midlife transition. By listening to the stories of others who had managed to navigate that passage successfully, I was able to appropriate some of their experience for myself. I was able to establish some markers, if not a specific map, for myself. And by looking through the lens of type, I was also able to discover some markers to suggest to others whose personality structures differ from my own. It is my hope that this will happen again for the stage that follows midlife. The experiences and suggestions I offer cannot map the coming to age journey for any of us, but they may offer some markers to aid us as we navigate our own journeys and perhaps help others do the same.

Midlife markers have been suggested by my work and by the work of many others. Coming to age markers are also being suggested by many gerontologists, psychologists, and sociologists, though their writings often concentrate on losses and dysfunctions. These writings also frequently focus on issues such as social security, health care, and adequate housing, which, as important and necessary as they are, do not always answer the cries of the spirit coming to age. I wanted to know more about the experience of people who have their basic needs met and are living successfully in their sixties and seventies. I wanted to know how they make meaning out of their lives.

I began to try to pull together my thoughts about and experiences with this life stage, and again, armed with a tape recorder and a legal pad, I set out to ask questions of people I thought could help move my own thinking along. I hoped they might be able to identify another marker or two for the coming to age journey. I asked many questions:

- How have you navigated to this point?
- What has been—and what is—your traveling gear?
- What gives you joy now?
- What concerns you most?
- How have you changed over the years?
- What, if anything, has held you back?
- What are you most happy that you have changed?
- How do you feel about your work—both the activity tied to production that we often call work, and the work of coming to age?
- How do you now relate to yourself, to others, and to the universe?
- Are you able to live authentically, and do you have some sense of comfort in the world you inhabit?

- Do you see a meaningful pattern when you look back over your life?

- Do you see your story as related to a story larger than your own?

I chose to concentrate on people living creatively with some sense of purpose, meaning, and intentionality. I could have focused on those who are not living creatively. We all know people who are not coming to age gracefully, and we can sometimes learn what we do not want to be and do by observing them. However, I suggest that it is more productive, if one is looking for guides for a journey, to look toward those who know something of the way that is desired.

We all recognize people coming to age without creativity, consciousness, and a sense of adventure. C. G. Jung (1981), founder of analytical psychology and theorist behind the MBTI personality inventory, tells us that people who don't age creatively—who don't come to know themselves and who try to live in later life by the rules of early life—are in danger of becoming "hypochondriacs, niggards, pedants, applauders of the past or else eternal adolescents . . ." (par. 786). Or as Roger Gould (1981) warns us, "When blocked for too long we become negative, sour joy killers dwelling on our inadequacies, consumed with envy and blaming others because we can't admit the powerful split within us" (p. 57).

We know, often too well, what can happen to us as we age, even in the most favorable circumstances with adequate income and good health. We see it all around us. We know aging people whose most interesting conversation deals with their latest bodily malfunction. We know what happens when we cling too long to the past. We see men (and some women as well) clinging to the hero myth. They continue, in varying degrees, to try to dominate and conquer, well past the time when this was an appropriate approach. We see women (and some men as well) lacking the ability to claim their own lives, instead remaining dependent and passive well past the time when such childish behavior was appropriate or necessary. We see people hanging on to their work, their children, their titles, their possessions, and their childhood faith for a sense of identity and security beyond the point when identity can be provided by such attachments. We see aging people continuing to let culture define who they are, spending great amounts of time, energy, and money trying to preserve a youthful appearance, without realizing the illusion of depending on this for a sense of worth. We see the tightening of the jaw and the hardening of staunchly held opinions in an attempt to ward off ambiguity and paradox and to preserve the status quo and some sense of certainty and safety. We see the inability of people coming to age to be alone without loneliness, and we see the pain of isolation when they cannot connect with themselves, their culture, or those around them. These behaviors abound in our time, in our culture, and sometimes in ourselves as well. And while this book will not deny them, we will be looking through another lens. We will focus on those people who, though certainly not perfectly or without struggle, are aging with vitality, contentment, generosity, spaciousness, connectedness, relatedness, joy, and devotion. We will look for the gifts that can emerge from the experience of six or seven decades.

In part 1 of this book, we will look at the period of coming to age—the time beyond the midlife transition. In chapter 1, we will explore briefly the nature of creative living in the later years—primarily in the sixties and seventies—touching on the areas of work, relationships, and spiritual growth.

In chapter 2, we will look at what one person called "the fruition of the long term." Here we will attempt to see how people deal with the primary psychological and spiritual tasks of the coming to age period, the making of meaning out of their long lives, and the preparation for leaving when the time is right.

In chapter 3, we will look through the lens of Jungian psychology at the process of adult development, type theory, and particularly type development theory, to see what that theory can contribute to our understanding of the coming to age period.

In the first four chapters of part 2 (chapters 4 through 7), we will explore more explicitly the coming to age period in the context of the different MBTI types, and, when possible, through the words of creative people coming to age. I have chosen, for the sake of simplicity and in an attempt to be true to Jung's type theory, to group the material using Jung's mental function categories (NF, ST, NT, and SF) with reference to individual types within these categories. In these chapters, I will share the stories of creative people with different personality preferences as they speak of their lives in the coming to age period. I will also tentatively suggest some particular challenges that people in each category must meet and some particular gifts that they often find have been saved for their later years. The particular challenges that I suggest for each category are not necessarily at home only in the category in which I have housed them, but are especially and particularly present there. The gifts that I suggest for each type also are not necessarily restricted to the type in which I place them, but are especially important to that group because they can rarely be obtained by people in that category without the benefit of many years of living. They are truly gifts reserved for the later years for those people.

The last chapter (chapter 8) will highlight some of the struggles, victories, and learnings that each of the MBTI types might wish to share with those who follow them. Neither the people interviewed nor I have any formulas for creative aging, but they, as one person said, are glad "to shout down the hall" what they have come to know.

In an attempt to communicate this material, I will share my experiences and those of the people interviewed for this book in a conversational manner. The interview material that I report is a careful reconstruction of life journeys reported by people with different type codes. In each case, I have attempted to preserve the flavor and the exact words of the person being interviewed, while selecting segments of his or her dialogue. Through the interview material, I invite you to meet these creative people who are coming to age. I hope you will see each one as a beautiful portrait of a creative life, and that you will notice and appreciate the differences and the similarities of different paths. I hope you will learn from them as I have, and that we may all know the value of what we are discovering, while recognizing that we have only begun this process. I hope we will again realize the value of the clear and practical MBTI model, while remembering that no human experience can be entirely captured by this or any other model.

ACKNOWLEDGMENTS

If it takes a village to raise a child, it takes a group of creative, compassionate, articulate people who have lived full, long lives to write a book of this nature. I wish to express my great admiration and gratitude to the people who have shared the experiences of their bountiful lives so graciously in this book. I hope I have been able, at least at times, to convey the beauty of their stories. In addition, I wish to thank all those people coming to age creatively whom I cannot name but whose lives have crossed my personal and professional path and who may feel themselves present in this book. They are indeed present.

I also want to especially thank Katharine Myers, who not only has supported me abundantly in my work on this book but is showing me personally what it means to come to age creatively. I am also grateful to her for supporting the MBTI's coming to age by her work on the developmental aspects of type.

And last, I want to offer heartfelt thanks to Cindy Bowers, Catherine Fitzgerald, Joan Garrabrant, Margaret Hartzler, B. Millner, Naomi Quenk, and Tish Paschall, who read and offered valuable feedback in the rough draft stages of this book; to Jeanne Schlesinger, who demonstrated a great deal of patience as she forced a computer to produce in spite of me; and to Melinda Adams Merino, Jill Anderson-Wilson, Kathy Hummel, and the staff at Davies-Black Publishing, who set me free to write my own book.

. . . they pursue meaninglessness

until they force it to mean.

—Rollo May, *The Courage to Create*

PART 1

COMING TO AGE

*P*eople coming to age creatively have successfully navigated the midlife transition, whenever it occurred in their lives. They know, whatever the circumstances, that their transitions have been meaningful. Looking back, though almost never in the midst of the process, people see that the midlife passage was an invitation to live fully. They recognize that the transition was a call to acknowledge and cherish gifts that have been reserved for their later years. They recognize it to have been an invitation to renew their lives and grow into the full, authentic people they were created to be, and, in fact, always have been, *in potentia.*

In retrospect, they acknowledge that it was also an invitation to death—of outgrown activity and an outgrown sense of identity. For these creative people coming to age, the archetype of death and rebirth, which rests at the center of much of the religious wisdom of the world, often has worn a personal face. Most life transitions, in fact, are about death and rebirth in that they usually require change and the letting go of outgrown things in order to embrace new possibilities; however, the midlife transition is often different in intensity and in purpose. What is let go of, what is sacrificed in the midlife transition is one's ego-dominated way of perceiving oneself and of being in the world. These old ego-centered ways are sacrificed to deeper, more complete and authentic ways of perceiving and being, usually over a significant period of time. In retrospect, although rarely when they are occurring, these sacrifices are seen as willing sacrifice.

The concept of willing sacrifice requires that we, when necessary, relinquish something good for something better. When we are required to willingly sacrifice and we cannot find meaning in this, we will suffer. The suffering, the misery, the stuckness—as well as the acting out that often accompanies midlife—are often caused by our inability or refusal to sacrifice that which has served us well in order to embrace that which can serve us better. We hang on to old concepts of ourselves or old ways of being and find life stagnant and sterile, or we exhaust ourselves with meaningless activity defending against these feelings of stagnation and sterile emptiness. In a real sense, when we are called to and cannot participate in willing sacrifice, we choose death over life, as expressed by Parker J. Palmer (1990) in the following passage:

> Death in various forms is sometimes comforting, while resurrection and new life can be demanding and threatening. If I lived as if resurrection were real, and allowed myself to die for the sake of new life, what might I be called upon to do? (p. 142)

Questions about what I am called to be or to do and what this might mean to the life structure and relationships I have built are questions that can send a shiver of fear through most of us, as well as a tingle of undeniable excitement. To fail to acknowledge these questions or to anesthetize ourselves to the discomfort they bring—as we often do with addictions, overwork, overconsumption, relationship infidelities, and other creative defenses—is to refuse the invitation to a vital coming to age period of life.

Yet to concentrate simply upon the fear and the possible stagnation of the middle passage is as ridiculous as speaking only of the labor pain of childbirth without speaking of the baby. The people who speak in this book have recognized the baby. They have chosen life. They have moved through the middle passage in many different ways and with different degrees of ease or difficulty. It has certainly been easier for some than for others, but few have moved with consistent gracefulness. Many have had to make soul-wrenching decisions. Some have sustained crises in their sense of self, and some have sustained crises in relationships, in work, and in their belief systems. None of them is immune to future conflict. Yet they have all chosen life. And because they have chosen life, so can their children, their mates, their co-workers, their neighbors, and their culture. Let us look at and listen now to a few things they might have to say about the process of the midlife transition and the period that follows it. Let us notice how they wrest meaning from their lives and discover the beautiful integrity of their experiences. Let us explore how some understanding of type and type development can aid us as we look at different paths toward life in the coming to age period.

CHAPTER 1

MOVING BEYOND MIDLIFE

Aging does not need to be hidden or
denied, but can be understood, affirmed
and experienced as a process of growth
by which the mystery of life is slowly
revealed to us.

—Henri Nouwen and Walter Gaffney,
Aging: The Fulfillment of Life

$\mathcal{W}$e all know older people, al-
though fewer than we might wish, for whom the mystery of life does
seem to be revealing itself, and we also know older people who find
their later years marked by fear, regret, and bitterness. The former
group of people, though they may volunteer few "answers" to life's mys-
teries, are people we want to speak with. They know something of the
frailty of human life and the limits of human endeavors, yet they do not
despair. They exude a sense of inner authority, but rarely impose this on
others. They take responsibility for their lives and set others free to take
responsibility for theirs. They attend to the everyday needs of their bodies, lives, and communities, but they are not tyrannized by the demands
of the physical world. They work, but without drivenness, and no longer
need to constantly impress others with their accomplishments or their
youthfulness. They are freer and more playful than many of their peers.

As much as we desire to spend time with such people, sometimes it is also hard to be in their presence. It is easy to fall into idolizing or envying them because we feel unworthy and fear their judgment or our own. It is also easy to feel disconnected from them. They invite us into our own fullness, but we cannot connect with them through our victimhood. If we can allow them to be our guides, they can challenge us without bitterness. They can encourage us to find our own journey map, and they can love us for our gifts and forgive us for our shortcomings. They can help us keep our eyes on the treasure of the journey while never losing sight of the dragons that sit by the side of the road.

Who are these people? How did they get to this place? Almost without exception, these creative people coming to age have passed through the fire. Let us look briefly at the fire of midlife transition and the time beyond it.

MIDLIFE TRANSITION

Does midlife ever end? How many times this agonizing question has been heard from a student in the back of a class on midlife, from an individual in a counseling session, or from a participant in a weekend retreat on midlife transition. It may translate into common midlife questions such as these:

- What is life about?
- What am I missing in my life?
- Have I made the right choices?
- Is it too late to make new choices?
- What if I were to make a mistake at this stage of my life?
- Who else will my decisions affect?

These are the questions of those for whom this midlife transition has been, in the words of the popular song "The Rose," "too lonely" and "too long." People are frequently worn down and wearied by all the demands of a midlife transition. They are often tired and disoriented, even if sometimes energized and excited as well, by what Murray Stein (1977) in his book *In Midlife: A Jungian Perspective,* calls the stages of *separation* and *liminality* in the midlife transition. In *Navigating Midlife*

(Corlett and Millner, 1993), my coauthor and I looked extensively at the experiences of people with different MBTI type codes in this stage as well as in the subsequent stage of reintegration. The reintegration stage is often much less difficult for people, as the disorientation of the transition begins to subside and life begins to take a new form more appropriate for later life. However, for those in the earlier stage of the transition, "Does it ever end?" is a question much in need of a response.

> *Midlife transition sometimes sneaks up on people.*

Midlife transition sometimes sneaks up on people. It can announce itself with a vague sense of disquiet and questioning or the awareness of a few wrinkles that weren't present yesterday. Or it can arrive with a great deal more force and be marked by feelings of stagnation, despair, isolation, and loneliness. Many people, when they look back, can name marker events that initiated the transition—such things as deaths, job losses, and relationship changes.

In the earliest stage of midlife, the stage Stein (1977) calls *separation,* many people are haunted by feelings of discontent, frustration, boredom, anxiety, and restlessness. Some find themselves feeling their lives are out of control. Others feel their lives are too constricted. Some feel they have arrived at midlife without accomplishing what they had hoped. Others feel they have arrived having accomplished what they desired and wondering why the rewards don't feel more satisfying. Many are facing losses of one kind or another: the death of a parent, adult children leaving home, breakups in relationships, loss of career, loss of a sense of security. Some experience for the first time an awareness that time is running out, although, in truth, midlife people generally have a lot of time left. Many feel for the first time the loss of youth, young bodies, and limitless energy. Some find that their childhood faith is insufficient. And almost all feel that they must do something to revitalize themselves and prevent the second half of life from being a stale replay of the first. Most recognize Peggy Lee's perplexity when she sings, "Is that all there is?"

The middle period, which Stein calls *liminality,* is that time when one is betwixt and between and may feel pulled and even torn in opposite directions. People at this stage want to move ahead with their lives and make changes because they know that this is where excitement and a sense of renewal are, but they also want to be secure and undisturbed.

They often know there are things they want to do and changes they want to make, but they may fear the cost. They sense they have become alienated from their true selves. They know they have not been able to develop all aspects of themselves and often feel these undeveloped parts crying out for inclusion. The answer to the healthy midlife question, Is this all there is? is usually no. There is, in fact, often a great deal more life to be lived, and the missing part—the part waiting to be lived—is the part that has been overlooked or sacrificed. Many midlife people have become very accomplished at meeting the needs dictated by their environment, and often this has been done at some personal cost. They may have become expert managers of enterprises only to find that they have done so to the exclusion of allowing time for their own inner development. They may find that they have nurtured and cared for their communities and families at the expense of their own care and nurture. They may find that the creative activity that gave them so much pleasure in their youth has been laid aside and in some cases literally forgotten for several decades.

These modern midlife people may wonder if they have made the correct choices and may agonize over the cost (and the promise) of now making new choices. They often realize they have lost their sense of creativity, spontaneity, and joy, and may have forgotten how to play. Often they have outgrown their childhood faith, if they had one, and have found their religious institutions unwilling or unable to assist them in finding their sense of personal meaning and their place in the larger scheme of creation. Sometimes people in midlife make destructive choices. They commonly err in one of two directions: Either they do not see the value of what they have developed and the need to hold onto that while they integrate what they have missed, or they are too stuck and fearful to risk allowing their undeveloped life to have any place at all at their psyche's table.

Not all midlife transitions may be as difficult as I have described. For each individual, the nature of the transition depends on all that has preceded it in that person's life as well as on the individual's personal resources and support systems. Our culture, as well as our families, often encourages us to stray from our true selves—to develop our false selves, if you will. Midlife transition is most difficult for people who have not been able to develop and lead their lives in harmony with their true selves and who find themselves in an imposed transition period without a strong sense of themselves or a supportive environment.

Yet often there is also struggle for people who *have* lived their essential nature in early life. They frequently find themselves in midlife successful and affirmed by their families and their culture. And they frequently discover that they are securely tethered to the "status quo," even in the face of internal and external demands for change. Clinging to the status quo, as pleasing as it may seem, exacts a price. Denial of the demand for growth can lead to diminishing energy and creativity and increasing depression. It can also deny the meaning of one's life. The middle passage is about change. As Jung (1981) warns us, "We cannot live the afternoon of life according to the programme of life's morning. . . . Whoever carries over into the afternoon the law of the morning . . . must pay for it with damage to his soul . . ." (par. 784, 787).

Trying to live later life according to the rules of earlier life is dangerous not only for the individual's soul but for the culture's soul as well. We live in a culture that does not know how to age. We have few individual or cultural role models for growing older, and as a result, people do not want to acknowledge that they are past midlife. As long as we as a culture cannot envision a graceful post-midlife period, people in their middle years will resist moving into this life stage. This will not only disallow them the joys of moving on, but, unfortunately, will block the younger generation from growing up as well. And if the younger generation can see no way to move into the fullness of later life, we may then expect that they will continue to act as adolescents, sometimes lacking commitment and a sense of responsibility, blocked from moving into their adulthood by those who do not know how to move on to a conscious and creative later life.

So to the question, Does midlife transition ever end? I answer yes. Midlife transition can and usually does end. I can say this with confidence, for I have experienced the process, and I have watched many others who have also experienced it. The middle passage often

> *If the younger generation can see no way to move into the fullness of later life, we may then expect that they will continue to act as adolescents.*

ends very quietly. As one midlife person put it, "You would have thought when midlife was over there would have been fireworks, considering all its traumas. But it just faded away."

Stein also defines a later stage of midlife transition, the stage of *reintegration.* In the reintegration stage, lives shift and people move on.

Often people are surprised to find the transition waning, and they may not know what caused the shift. Sometimes observable changes such as career shifts, geographic moves, and relationship changes have been made. Often more subtle and less observable shifts in attitude, behavior, and balance have been made. People find they are in some ways the same as they were before the transition and at the same time quite different.

The midlife transition often ends with the feeling that things are coming together. The intensity and the questions so urgently asked have lost their energy. One feels more connected to one's authentic self and finds that at least sometimes the essential part of that self can communicate with the outside world. One knows that both the inner world and the outer world must be accommodated and that one must care for oneself and for others as well. One knows one's home base and therefore is more able to travel safely away from it when required. One sees darkness and light and finds them related. People come to know that they are alone, that no one can or will take care of them. Yet, paradoxically, they also know that they are not alone, but rather are connected quite mysteriously to others, to the universe, and often to the Divine as well.

The midlife transition has a purpose—to orient the individual to the afternoon of life. That orientation can be as varied as the individuals experiencing it. It may offer an individual work for the rest of life as it did C. G. Jung. Jung (1965) spoke of this period and its meaning for him in his autobiography, *Memories, Dreams, Reflections:*

> The years when I was pursuing my inner images were the most important in my life—in them everything essential was decided. It all began then; the later details are only supplements and clarifications of the material that burst forth from the unconscious and at first swamped me. It was the *prima materia* for a lifetime's work. (p. 199)

Midlife is also about the expansion of personality. It is about finding those parts of ourselves that we have not developed and integrating them. It is about finding those things that were ours to do but that we didn't address because we were too busy establishing a career, raising a family, and participating in our communities. It is about moving toward being more complete and whole people. And it is also about the meaning that comes to many when they recognize that their lives do have a pattern, and that this pattern has meaning and may be connected to a Pattern and a Meaning larger than their own personal histories.

Midlife transition requires time, space, and energy for reflection and is often demanded just at the time when these elements are least available. Most midlife people are busy and involved, and some are burdened and exhausted. The need to break away from the tyranny of the world, to discover—or rediscover—their own authentic individual meaning, and to develop all parts of themselves comes just at the time when the world's demands are most arduous and personality is most split. Yet the transition happens, as it must, in spite of culture—or perhaps because of culture. Midlife people, if they are to prepare for the next stage of life, must find their way back to themselves; from that place of authentic identity, they must reconnect in new and creative ways with their environment. That to which they reconnect may not seem the same as that which they left. Sometimes the reconnection is with different work and people, but often it is reconnection to the same work and people, known in a quite different way.

So what is this period after the subsiding of the midlife transition like? What can we say about this period when we have passed through the fire of midlife and have not yet come to the late-life transition of final letting go and leaving? How can we think of this period we call coming to age?

BEYOND MIDLIFE TRANSITION

As we come to age, we can begin to claim all of ourselves, find our place in the universe, and discover the joy, power, and freedom in doing so. Perhaps the best way to describe this period of life is through poetry. Poet May Sarton, in "Now I Become Myself," speaks of this period when she describes a time in which one can live all of one's self. She describes this as a time beyond the stage when one has "worn other people's faces" and "run madly, as if time were crying a warning." The power and the relief that can come to post-midlife people who now find that they can, in Sarton's words, "stand and claim their own lives" brings great joy.

Poet Mary Oliver, in "Wild Geese," expresses the joy and freedom and sense of connection post-midlife people can experience when they come to know that the world calls to them, acknowledging their "place in the family of things." That sense of joy, freedom, and connection was also expressed zestfully by a sixty-two-year-old man who declared, "I'm [now] perfectly comfortable in my universe."

This post-midlife period, which I call the coming to age period, can also be marked by more conscious living. The addition of years cannot guarantee conscious living or the acquisition of wisdom; however, if we can successfully navigate midlife and creatively engage the years that follow, conscious, creative, and fulfilling living may be the reward. This way of living is marked by greater awareness of the entirety of our authentic selves and of our place in the world around us. As we age, we discover—or create—mature communities in which people can support one another while allowing for individual differences. When lived creatively, this coming to age period can allow us to say with Sarton that we live all of ourselves and with Oliver that we have a place in the family of things.

The coming to age period is often marked by greater assurance and serenity than the midlife period that preceded it. In this period, we can come to know the difference between solitude and loneliness and often find that we are very fond of our own company. We learn to accept ambiguity, knowing that paradox is often the only truth there is and that many difficult questions will never be answered. We have come to know that we are limited, that we contain contradictions that we cannot work out, and, surprisingly, that we are not terribly bothered by this knowledge. We have learned that evil and good, both in the world and in ourselves, dwell side by side and are often hard to distinguish. Having come face to face with some of our own limitations, tolerance—if not acceptance—slips in. We know how terribly complicated it is to judge and sometimes decide we are not up to the task. Writer and psychotherapist Thomas Moore (1992) addresses this in *Care of the Soul:*

> *The coming to age period is often marked by greater assurance and serenity than the midlife period that preceded it.*

> Often care of the soul means not taking sides where there is a conflict at a deep level. It may be necessary to stretch the heart wide enough to embrace contradiction and paradox. (p. 14)

This period is frequently marked by a greater desire to express our true gifts, and sometimes we have more adequate resources with which to do this. Most people who come to age with awareness find that they are freer than ever before from expectations of parents and culture. If the midlife transition has been navigated well, it has allowed for some disengagement from unexamined mandates from family and culture and more confirmation of one's true self—one's real nature and essence. With this deeper self-knowledge, we can allow ourselves to evaluate what is offered by family and culture without having to either accept it wholeheartedly or rebel against it completely. We also often discover that we are freer of heavy parenting responsibilities and of work defined for us by others. As one person said, "I'm freer now, for there is nothing that I really need that I don't have." This is a comment from one who defines need from a place of deep understanding. She is very selective about what she calls a need, and this allows for a profound freedom almost never known to the young.

Vividness, sensuality, and sometimes sexuality characterize the coming to age period. Vividness comes because time is valued, not only because it is limited but also because there is uncertainty about the quality of the time that remains. Will illness intervene? In the light of this kind of awareness, the body is to be cared for, real friendships are to be grasped as the precious things they are, and the beauty of every day is to be cherished. As one person said, "Life is valued more when you realize you are on its slippery side."

The coming to age period is a time for humor—not at the expense of others, but rather in terms of taking oneself and others less seriously. It is, in a sense, about detachment, but with caring. Henry Nouwen, Roman Catholic priest and author, and Walter Gaffney, in *Aging: The Fulfillment of Life* (1990), say:

> Humor is knowledge with a soft smile. It takes distance but not with cynicism, it relativizes but does not ridicule, it creates space but does not leave you alone. (p. 74)

This time is marked by more conscious choice making. One is able to decide what is one's own and what belongs to others. And it is particularly because of this developing ability to know what is one's own that the post-midlife period is often marked by conscious commitment that comes from the soul and is offered freely. The ego, that conscious sense of ourselves that we develop when we are young and that allows us to live and prosper, is always evaluating how it is being received. The ego can rarely offer without demand for results and for acceptance by and affirmation from others. But as we age creatively and the ego becomes less tyrannical, we can

This time for vital involvement that feeds rather than depletes can be a time of great creativity.

sometimes offer simply because it is ours to offer, because it is our part in the family of humanity.

Carol Pearson (1991), in her book *Awakening the Heroes Within*, describes the life journey in terms of archetypal energy. In her model, it is the Seeker archetype, the seeking energy, that often initiates the midlife transition. The Seeker must go apart, ask the hard questions, and seek its own authentic way. But it is the Lover archetype—the energy of commitment and passion—that leads beyond the midlife passage. The midlife transition often fades when we discover the passion, the relationship, the work, the idea, the creative endeavor to which we can commit body and soul. The confusion and disorientation of the midlife journey fade when conscious choice making selects a new vision and commits to it with passion and hope.

Erik Erikson (1986), American psychologist and developmental theorist, writes in *Vital Involvement in Old Age* that the two later life stages, for successfully developing people, are marked by care and generativity and by integrity and wisdom. Successful post-midlife people are generative. They care deeply, and they offer the fruits of their life experiences to the next generation, often finding in so doing a sense of personal integrity. The work of this period, the sharing of one's wisdom, is what I believe Erikson means by *vital involvement,* that is, work that contributes but does not deplete the giver. People who see their lives as being generative and having integrity are saved from stagnation and a sense of despair, which, unfortunately, can be seen often in the lives of those unable to age gracefully.

This post-midlife period, this time for vital involvement that feeds rather than depletes, can be a time of great creativity. Whether or not the creative activity produces a product, it can produce a renewed sense of spontaneity, playfulness, and adventure. It often involves the post-midlife person in something new, and it almost always demands a sense of adventure and risk taking. It can be the building of a tool shed or the planting of a garden, the organization of a group or the writing of a poem. Whatever it is, it is done for the sake of one's soul. It is done because it is what one is "called" to do. It gives a sense of renewal, of joy, satisfaction, and self-expression. It also offers zest and purpose and meaning for life. It grows out of the self and brings joyful fruit to the world. And it can sometimes exhaust the person coming to age as well, as we shall see in the next section on work.

WORK

I'm not suggesting that old people not work,
but that they not be driven by a purpose.

—A. Guggenbuhl-Craig,
"Long Live the Old Fool"

All people coming to age *work*, in the most complete sense of the word. In fact, one of life's most significant tasks is accomplished as we simply learn to live creatively with age. It is indeed an accomplishment to complete a good life and therefore show the way to those who will follow. In many ways, the lines that separate the areas of living, working, and playing become less distinct as we age.

Many people in their sixties and seventies and beyond also continue to work within the more limited definition that defines work as activity producing a product or service. These people function in a variety of ways and for a range of purposes. Work can provide the necessary financial resources for survival or for "extras," as well as a sense of being useful, productive, and connected. Most working people coming to age would understand and agree with Guggenbuhl-Craig (1991) when he suggests they wish "not [to] be driven by a purpose," although not all would say they have mastered this injunction. They would advise that one try to have a sense of play about work. "Tell them to find something that is new and interesting for them to do," was advice offered by several of our creatively aging people to those who follow them. "Tell them to find something that they won't get tired of," advised another. Or, more directly, "Get a creative project!"

Perhaps nowhere more than in the area of work is the later life freedom I spoke of earlier more obvious. Many people are freer from financial and time restraints than they were in earlier life, and their work can be more freely chosen. People who have spent many years tied to work that did not "fit" them are particularly delighted to find the release that retirement can bring.

Edwin, retired for slightly longer than two years from the practice of dentistry, was quick to express his gratitude for having had the financial resources to be able to retire and for the delight in it he experiences each day. He spoke of the great happiness he feels now that he is released from a career that didn't fit.

Edwin had always planned to "get a profession." He had entered college with the intention of being a premed student but had graduated as an economics major. After a short stint in journalism and sales, where he "didn't sell much," he read in the newspaper want ads that a pharmacist could make $300 a week—a good salary in those days. This motivated him to head for the local pharmacy school admissions office. "To get to the pharmacy school, you had to walk down a long hall and then turn right. At the end of the hall, before you turned right toward the pharmacy school, was the dentistry school. So I just stopped there," he laughed, "and the rest is history." This story is not quite true, he admitted, but "it does make a good story." In fact, after finding that pharmacy school would take three years (rather than the two he had anticipated) for completion, he did stop by the dental school. Upon learning that becoming a dentist would require only one more year than becoming a pharmacist, he made his career choice—one that his mother would approve, he quickly pointed out with a wink.

The profession, unfortunately, was never a good fit. He explained: "It was never quite right. It was too small for my expansive personality, living in five rooms all day and looking in mouths. I loved my patients and they loved me, but it was not a good professional choice and I stayed too long. Retirement feels like being unshackled."

Many people, of course, have found their work to be a good fit. Often they continue this work in some form in their retirement years. This is particularly true for people in careers in which wisdom is recognized as a qualification for their work. As one person said, "I'm lucky to be in psychology. It is a field that ages well. In psychology you are more respected when you are older." Although the accumulation of years cannot ensure wisdom, the reflection on life experiences—and life wounds—can often bring wisdom and compassion to consciously aging people. This can be an invaluable aid in fields dealing with human development, such as psychology, counseling, teaching, ministry, and health care, as well as in creative endeavors.

Others who may wish to continue to work in the fields in which they were previously engaged might include women who spent early life nurturing families and entered the world of work late, or men and women who find great joy in mentoring younger colleagues. "The associates do the day-to-day work," said one man who now focuses on mentoring others. He has learned to let go and can now enjoy not only seeing his work live on but also relaxing while he observes it happening.

Many people in their sixties and seventies have restructured their work into what I call self-fulfilling projects. They have found the small pieces of their work that they love and have skillfully built them into masterpieces. They leave preaching and become spiritual directors; they leave teaching and form groups to introduce new and innovative science education to underprivileged school systems; they leave college administration and form institutes to encourage interfaith dialogue; they leave publishing and join programs to encourage children in the creative arts; they leave law and offer legal aid to those who can't pay; they leave secretarial jobs and write books.

Sometimes they are paid and sometimes they are not. One man I interviewed, who was not quite ready to retire when a corporate reorganization forced him out in his sixties, decided to create his own career. He had been working on a project for his company that the company felt it couldn't afford. He went home and set up his computer, and he is now completing the project on his own and will attempt to sell it back to the company. Self-creating careers is the rule rather than the exception for people in later life, and it is the freedom, the creativity, and the imagination of creatively aging people that make this possible.

> *Many have found the small pieces of their work that they love and have skillfully built them into masterpieces.*

Other people in their sixties and seventies find that the coming to age period provides them with the opportunity to do something they have always wanted to do. This is particularly true for people who have never found fulfillment in their work, or who gave up some special desire early in life in order to meet life's practical demands. These people often find that in the coming to age period, when they are less bound to work for production and recognition, they can make their most significant and lasting contributions.

When Betty's husband, whose military career had moved her around the world, retired, Betty found herself able to offer full-time volunteer effort to a cause fostering racial harmony and spiritual development. It was the first time in her life she had been able to do this meaningful work, and she had to struggle at times to "keep it in its place." She became so devoted to her work that she feared it might invade her personal and relational time.

A retired corporate executive expressed the consensus of many retired people: "Now I do what I want and I want what I do." Joseph, a retired military officer, expressed similar sentiments. When I called him to request an interview for this book, he explained to me that, although he would be happy to be interviewed, he had work that took precedence over the interview. "I can't talk on Mondays, Tuesdays, or Wednesdays," he informed me, "because I have to work helping my friend sell apples."

Often, but not always, the work is unpaid. Financial obligations have to be met, but often the amount of income required is lower than might be expected. As one woman who now works without pay expressed it, "I don't have a lot of money, but I have an apartment and I have some dresses. I can get books at the library. What I don't have now is a lot of time, and I don't want to sell much of it."

If work for these creative people coming to age is not primarily about income and recognition, it also is not something intended to "keep them occupied." It is often activity that comes from the soul, from the core of who they are—activity that originates in the person and is expressed in the world. It comes, as one person said, "from the inside out." This work is most often primarily about mastery rather than production, and about self-authority rather than pleasing others. It is about life meaning, authenticity, and purpose. It is often about expression of that passion that leads from midlife into the later years. When our work comes from the inside out and is not relied on for identity, power, and wealth, but rather is characterized by traits such as authenticity, self-authority, and personal passion, it is more significant. As one person said, "When I had no boss to pay me—or to fire me—I was able to do my real work." Many people coming to age have found that their real work, the work that comes from their souls, may be participating in the "creation of a more humane world."

In fact, when work is viewed as a *mission* or *passion,* people often sense a resurgence of energy. Again, this is Erikson's concept of vital involvement, which contributes but does not deplete the giver. It is what Joseph Campbell calls *following your bliss.* It resembles the Buddhist concept of *effortless effort.* This view of work is appropriate to people who may have less energy and less time, but who have a tremendous amount to offer if they don't deplete themselves in the effort.

Often this work of the soul can be done only after people can give up the need for producing a service or product that our culture (and their own egos) assures them will produce a desired result. Only when they can work without placing a personal claim on the work's outcome can they undertake the enormous, significant tasks that can really never be finished or bring approval and recognition. Parker Palmer (1990) tells such a story in *The Active Life:*

> I remember talking with a friend who has worked for many years at the Catholic Worker, a ministry to the poor in New York City. Daily she tries to respond to waves of human misery that are as ceaseless as surf in that community. Out of my deep not-knowing I asked her how she could keep doing a work that never showed any results, a work in which the problems keep getting worse instead of better. I will never forget her enigmatic answer: "The thing you don't understand, Parker, is that just because something is impossible doesn't mean you shouldn't do it! . . . I have never asked myself if I was being effective, but only if I was being faithful." (p. 76)

This soul work, wonderful as it is, can also be problematic. As one person said, "I knew I was aging when I noticed my mind promised things my body couldn't deliver." The enthusiasm and vision that can come from a successful midlife transition of contemplation and introspection can often drive people in their postmidlife years to exhaust themselves. People living consciously in the coming to age period of life learn to honor their bodies and to recognize limitations that physical aging tends to impose. Jungian analyst Helen Luke (1987) writes of the need for aging people to discover a spirit of discriminating wisdom that can separate moment by moment the wheat of life from the chaff (p. 19). Yet even when the wheat and the chaff have been separated, there is often a great deal of wheat left.

I, personally, being a lifelong workaholic, have found this separating of the wheat from the chaff to be one of the major tasks of my post-midlife period. A few years ago, I initiated the formation of a small non-profit group designed to assist people, as the mission statement says, "in living lives of creativity, meaning, and compassion." This vision is something I have a great commitment to developing in my own life, as well as to helping others to realize. The organization took on a life of its own. It quickly became a growing and demanding project, and I found myself devoting body and soul to the work, which felt like a repeat performance of the earlier part of my life. I became bone weary and unable to be either creative or truly compassionate because I was mired in myriad details and the heaviness of responsibility toward the wonderful group of other people involved in the project. My body, now in its mid-fifties, began to announce in dreams and in physical symptoms that it would no longer accommodate my overcommitment. There was a period in my life when I could handle overcommitment by staying up for a night or two to catch up. But this was no longer true. Yet I believed in the project and did not want to give up my commitment to this group.

One night I decided to explore this situation. I called together a *clearness committee*—a Quaker process in which one takes one's issue to a group of trained listeners who are committed to recognize the wisdom of the presenter's inner teacher and the help-fulness of a mature community that does not seek to give advice or press its own agenda. I hoped that the care and concern of the listeners and my own inner teacher would shed some new light on my issue. During my presentation, I made an offhand remark about a T-shirt my husband and I have that reads, "Whatever it takes." It was a shirt that grew out of an effort to inspire a work group during very difficult times. It suddenly dawned on me that this might be an inappropriate slogan for me at this time in my life. One of the listeners asked me what I would prefer the shirt to say. After some thought, I came up with the answer. I wanted the T-shirt to say, "I'm just working on my project."

> *"Whatever it takes" brings to mind a clenched fist; "working on my project" offers an open palm.*

Substituting "working on my project" for "whatever it takes" does not mean I will give up all my demanding projects. It doesn't mean I won't work hard. I am a dutiful and responsible person who has some difficulty separating hard work from goodness, and I will, in fact, probably work on my projects in some form for the rest of my life. Yet now there is a different feel. "Whatever it takes" brings to mind a clenched fist; "working on my project" offers an open palm. "Whatever it takes" sounds like a threat, a demand for immediate effort; "working on my project" is a promise and allows a lifetime for completion. The shift is one of attitude from willfulness and requirement toward acceptance and devotion. One is heavy, the other light. And the lighter, more flowing, less demanding attitude is much more appropriate to my coming to age, although this may not be true for some who are more relaxed by temperament.

Another message about lightness and attitude shifts has come through my experience with yoga. After more than five years in the practice, I have a glimpse of what it means for me. Yoga is about going with the flow—not something that comes easily to me. Veniyoga, the particular discipline I practice, incorporates a slow, gentle recognition that "if it hurts, you aren't ready to do it." It teaches that the breath can carry you where you need to go. In coming to age, it is good to find where the breath, the spirit, the inner force can carry you. Then you can do almost anything without depletion and exhaustion.

I was relieved to learn that this same issue had arisen in the lives of others and in the life of one with a great deal of consciousness. C. G. Jung (1973), who as you may recall announced in *Memories, Dreams, Reflections* that his midlife transition had given him the material for his lifetime work, wrote the following at age sixty-seven:

> As one grows older one must try not to work oneself to death unnecessarily. At least that's how it is with me. . . . I can scarcely keep pace and must watch out that the creative forces do not chase me around the universe in a gallop. (pp. 320–321)

In one sense, physical limitations aid the process of consciousness, for they force us to stop chasing around the universe at a gallop. These limitations may require that we come to recognize and honor our bodies by supplying them with a more consciously chosen diet, more rest, more exercise, and more relaxation. They may require that we learn to play and to carry the yoke lightly. Physical limitations may also aid consciousness because they require that choices be made with more awareness. They slow us down—if only to make us find our glasses or keep from falling down the steps—and in the slowing down, they may provide us with more opportunity to wonder why we are doing what we are doing, why we are spending time with the people we are spending time with, and how we are to live in the coming to age period.

This is, perhaps, what Teilhard de Chardin (1960) means when he speaks of "the divinization of our passivities" (p. 67). Teilhard de Chardin is speaking not simply of accepting hardships and retiring from life, but of actively engaging limitations and using them to increase understanding and to transform personality to a deeper and richer level. Diminishments may act as teacher to people coming to age. As one woman said, "My body took me to sixty and got me to a safe place, and then it quit. It put me to bed for a while. I had some dizziness and could have gone from doctor to doctor. But I knew what I needed. I needed to underschedule."

When the time comes to separate not only the wheat from the chaff but the *best* wheat from the good wheat, we may learn something from the concept of willing sacrifice or the idea that "the good is often the enemy of the best." People consciously living their coming to age period may find themselves, as Jung did, in tremendous demand. A great deal of consciousness is required to know what good must be willingly sacrificed in order to move toward the better.

RELATIONSHIPS

"About loving I have little to learn
from the young."

—May Sarton, *Journal of a Solitude*

As conscious people coming to age, we may make fewer demands that things in general, and particularly relationships, go our way. As one person said, "I stopped demanding that the weather, my children, and the universe do what I want them to do."

We cannot stop demanding of others and contaminating our relationships with these demands until we know that we can rely on ourselves. Early life relationships are often built on what psychologists call *projection*. This action denies relationship with our true selves and affects our relationships with others as well. In psychological projection, as with a slide projector, we project out what is within. With slides and a projector, we project a picture onto a screen; what we see on the screen is really in the projector. We do the same thing when we project onto another person. We see in that individual what is really in ourselves. We are then free to love or to hate that person without having to love or hate the parts of ourselves we can see only in the other. For people in the process of becoming conscious, projection is one of the psyche's most exquisite teaching tools, even though it denies the other person her or his own identity. When we find ourselves overreacting to others and demanding that they do what we want them to, we might suspect that we are projecting. The task of consciously aging people is to stop projecting—to stop demanding that the weather,

> *The task of consciously aging people is to stop projecting—to stop demanding that the weather, the children, and the universe do what they want them to do.*

the children, and the universe do what they want them to do. It is a goal that is more often aspired to than reached.

Early in life we are often attracted to or repelled by people based on what we project onto them. In positive projections, we see in another person what we believe we do not have within ourselves; if the traits we project are desirable, we often attempt to acquire them by establishing a relationship with that person. For example, if we are shy and practical, we may find ourselves very attracted to someone who is outgoing and imaginative. Folklore recognizes this when it speaks of "opposites attracting." Or we may believe another person has something we desire and can receive only through her or him. For example, we may find a person like one of our parents, and we may form a relationship with that person hoping that she or he will give us what our parent was unable to provide. A woman may seek out a man very like her father and try to obtain from him a sense of approval and intimacy that her own father could not offer, or a man may look for a woman who can give him the nurturing he felt his mother was unable to give.

Commitment to our own growth can save us from this kind of projection and contamination of relationships. Increasing self-understanding— of both our dark and light sides—allows us to be and do what we were created to be and do, as well as to permit the others in our lives the same privilege.

Yet personal growth can be difficult and sometimes can cause disruption in relationships, particularly when one partner's increased self-awareness is not matched by equal growth in the self-awareness of the other. One woman in her sixties knew this well. In her early forties, she had returned to work and established a new set of friends and a new sense of herself. Her deep need for acknowledgment of these changes was summarized in this mandate to her husband of twenty-some years: "I can't be who you expect anymore, so get to know me." He couldn't do that and she couldn't continue to play the role—composed mainly of projections—their relationship had assigned her. The marriage did not survive: As she explained with some sorrow and a great deal of resignation, "He wanted his old wife and I had outgrown the part."

Often it is through the fire of the midlife transition that self-aware people begin to notice that expecting another person, beloved as she or he may be, to complete them, take care of them, and make them happy not only is going to be unsuccessful but also is unfair to another human being.

As author Gloria Steinem (1992) says, "When we look for a missing part of ourselves in other people we blot out their uniqueness" (p. 274). As we develop who we truly are, we can stop making as many demands on others. One woman in her seventies described her experience: "I've given up trying to influence others. I depend on myself, not on others or on organizations, for challenge." Creatively aging people come to know that the role of others in their lives is not to ensure their happiness, and that it is not their role to make the others in their lives happy. It feels like a great relief.

Instead of relying on others, creative people coming to age learn that what they find attractive or unattractive in other people is really what they want to develop or heal in themselves. Creative people coming to age can then accept, and sometimes come to love, other people as they really are. Or as one seventy-year-old said, "I'm finally coming to take people just as they are, not as I wish they were. It improves relationships."

Indeed it does improve relationships—with spouses, lovers, adult children, friends, and colleagues. On good days, some people in their sixties and seventies can proclaim the ultimate freedom in relationship as this person did: "I know I'm totally free to be myself and to allow you the same privilege when I can truly say I want nothing that you have. This does not mean I don't want you; quite the contrary. But I don't want what you have." It is a love that, as May Sarton knew, cannot be learned from the young.

Committing to one's own growth and fostering the growth of the other are not mutually exclusive. The poet Rainer Rilke (1987), in *Letters to a Young Poet*, defined love as the capacity of two solitudes to "protect and border and greet each other" (p. 78). This kind of relationship requires understanding, wisdom, and patience. It does not require that we always approve of the actions of the other or that they approve of ours.

As we take responsibility for our own growth and allow others to do the same, we can relate freely without need, without burdening responsibility, and without guilt to those who cross our paths and enrich our lives. And we may find the comfort of mature love. Author Gail Sheehy (1995) writes, "The comfort of mature love is the single most important determinant of older men's outlook on life" (p. 384). But it is not only men who come to appreciate the comforts of mature love, as illustrated by a woman describing her forty-five years of marriage:

> Friends are fun, but I love being with just the two of us. We can talk or not talk. We're relaxed and we're comfortable. No big productions. . . . This isn't because we're interested in the same things. I know nothing of his work, nor he of mine, but we do love music, theater, and travel together.

Happy retirement, long-term marriages, and friendships do not seem to depend on similarity of personality, doing things together, or even mutual interests, although it seems important to find some common interests. One woman married forty years put it well: "My husband and I are almost opposites. . . . I'm not going to change him and I don't try. If I want to do something, I can do it alone or with friends. He doesn't have to do everything with me."

But long-term marriages do seem to depend on commitment. A sixty-nine-year-old woman who has counseled many people with relationship difficulties over her long career, and has herself been married to the same man for forty-three years, had this to say:

> Those with long-term marriages have clear expectations that their marriages will be successful. . . . We learn that other people can't make us happy. We learn that only we, ourselves, are responsible for our happiness—no, that's the wrong word—for our *contentment*. Contentment has a lot to do with accepting oneself and one's mate with all the good and all the bad.

Commitment is, of course, not limited to marriage. Most lasting relationships with lovers, children, colleagues, and friends depend on commitment.

Relationships with friends are treasured by creative people coming to age. True friends in the coming to age period, it would appear, are not selected, as is often true in earlier life, by their proximity, their role in society, their blood ties, or even their common interests. They are not selected primarily by occupational or sexual alliances. They are selected most often by the way in which they accept us and the time they commit to being present for us. This is important to everyone, obviously, but it is often particularly important for prominent people who treasure those with whom they do not have to play roles or be wise, perfect, happy, or righteous. One woman spoke of her devotion to a group of women who have been meeting continually for twenty years and who share this kind of intimacy:

In the coming to age period, friends are selected most often by the way in which they accept us and the time they commit to being present for us.

> This group of women is one of the most important things in my life. We get together regularly—every Saturday—and no one misses unless she is sick or out of town. We know each other, both the good and the not-so-good, and we care about each other. We care about each other's lives, and we can talk about sad things that others may not want to hear about. Sometimes we cry and we laugh, too. We laugh a lot.

Long-term marriages have to do not only with comfortable intimacy, acceptance, and commitment, but also with sensuality, sexuality, and romance for many creatively aging people. Intimacy seems to thrive when it is not as blocked by roles and role expectations as it often is in the earlier years. Both men and women refer to the joy of sexuality in the sixties and seventies. Leisure and an attitude of playfulness can enrich sexuality. One seventy-four-year-old retired male executive explains, "The body is a little slower and sexual arousal takes a little longer, but it is still delicious." And a single woman in her sixties expressed a joy not uncommon for postmenopausal women: "Tell the younger women that life is more carefree after menopause. It's good for sex."

And there is the joyful coming together of those who have learned how to be apart. One woman, married forty-six years and separated several times from her husband by work requirements, speaks of the joy of being together:

> We guard our relationship. We've been separated and not by choice. It has helped me become independent, but it has also taught me that I don't need separate vacations. We have a date every Friday evening, and almost everyone knows that nothing can get in the way of that. My marriage is my first priority.

Relationships with adult children are improved, too, by some degree of "benign neglect," even as connection with them is treasured. This lack of a need to control does not mean that parents always approve of everything their adult children do. Comments such as "I ask my children questions, but I try not to pry," or "I don't try to make things happen with my children, although I do try to remember what it was like to be thirty" characterize these relationships. In the interviews, I noticed that most creative people coming to age had made some peace with their adult children. And those who were not able to had found some peace through their grandchildren, through those they mentored, or by assisting needy children.

Creative people coming to age also speak of the limits of relationships and of love. They know that no one can ever truly understand another or be understood by another. Some people speak of this as the "human condition"; others speak of it as a spiritual issue. "We can never be truly understood by another, save God Himself," said one man. And one woman said: "The realization of the difficulty of this task of loving others as they are has led me to some understanding of 'miserable sinner' language. . . . I can't do it [love others as they are]. It's too hard, and I'm forgiven over and over when I fail." These people realize the difficulty—if not the impossibility—of loving.

Forgiveness is important to people coming to age. In fact, parents I interviewed often spoke of asking forgiveness of their adult children. Creatively aging people have often come to terms with the midlife awareness that Levinson (1978) calls the *destruction/creation polarity* (p. 197), and nowhere is this more clearly seen than in their parenting. As one man said, "Parents who do not think they are in need of forgiveness from their children must be unconscious." And forgiveness is more than merely accepting. Forgiveness is about recognizing damage done, suffering it, and moving on. Helen Luke (1987) broadens this sentiment to include more of the younger generation than just one's own children:

> If an old person does not feel his need to be forgiven by the young, he or she certainly has not grown into age, but merely fallen into it and his or her blessing would be worth nothing. (p. 27)

The paradox seems to be that only as we see ourselves in need of forgiveness are we able to forgive others. Sometimes people coming to age are amused at the silliness of holding grudges against their own parents, particularly when their parents are old and ill. One man articulated this: "When you see your father unable to feed himself, it seems a bit ridiculous to pull up all the times he put you down. He can't hurt you now. It will be better for him and for you to just love him. This helps you, for he must accept your forgiveness just as you must forgive and as you must accept the forgiveness of others." One woman said more succinctly: "We must put up with and endure each other." And usually forgiveness can be accepted without excessive guilt, as shown in one man's statement about his relationship with his grown children:

> I'm a failure in some ways and I can't fix that, but I've learned to live with it. I've talked to my kids and owned some of my faults. I wish it were better, but I don't kick myself around anymore.

And it helps if we can put up with and endure each other with a little humor. "You can't go through fifty-two years of marriage without looking stupid, so you might as well laugh," says one woman.

So perhaps we can stop demanding and instead aspire to a different kind of love, described by this seventy-two-year-old man: "Finally,

I hope that people will remember that I loved them, and I hope the love was genuine, not manipulative, or false, or pretentious. I hope I can love and not cling to that which is loved." This is a sentiment aspired to, if not always attained by, creative people coming to age.

But perhaps there is also another kind of relationship that transcends ties to oneself and to others. Perhaps there is the possibility of relationship to Something beyond one's self and those others in one's life.

SPIRIT

"Among all my patients in the second half of life—that is to say, over thirty-five— there has not been one whose problem in the last resort was not that of finding a religious outlook on life."

—C. G. Jung,
Modern Man in Search of a Soul

Just as love and work appear to be the major components of the first half of life, spirit may be the major component of the second. What does it mean to find a religious outlook such as Jung suggests is necessary for people aging creatively? It certainly had nothing to do, in his mind, with membership in any religious organization or adhering to any creed. Rather, Jung (1965, p. 326) writes of religious outlook as having to do with relationship to the infinite. Religious outlook is concerned with seeing that one's own life has meaning and purpose and is related to and part of a Larger Plan or, as is often said, with seeing that our own small stories are related to a Large Story, usually in a most mysterious way.

Many, though not all, of the people interviewed for this book seem to have some sense that they are connected to Something. Most are, however, unable or unwilling to elaborate on It. Their reticence seems to stem from a distrust of expounding upon things they have only glimpsed and a fierce determination not to claim partial truth as Truth. In general, they rely little on general religious formulations, but they often appropriate formulations and adapt them to their own particular ways of seeing. Some are heavily committed to their churches and synagogues and many participate in religious activity, although they often speak of their beliefs in very particular and often personal ways. Some have no religious institutional affiliation. Many are comfortable with Mystery. Most are content to live with what they have come to see as unanswerable questions, and some have stopped asking these kinds of questions.

When speaking of spirituality, the conversation of many people drifted toward discussion of religious institutions, even though they sometimes denied their interest in the institutions they were talking about. Unlike midlife people, these creative people coming to age are rarely locked in significant conflict with religious institutions, although some have abandoned them altogether. Some find comfort in their institutions, especially in the community they provide and, interestingly, in the silence and the music that accompany worship. Comments such as the following are not uncommon: "My church community is my family," or "I'm not very religious, I guess, but I enjoy church. I enjoy the beauty and being with my son and his family, and I enjoy the music." Others coming to age are disillusioned with institutions, and statements such as "I hope I never hear another sermon" were also not uncommon. A few might even agree with Abraham Maslow (1970), who in his critique of organized religion suggests that it can be the enemy of genuine religious experience (p. 33). Most common, however, is an attitude of acceptance of what institutions can and cannot do. This sentiment was expressed well by one man who, with a slight shrug of his shoulders, said, "Sometimes spoken ministry is important or provocative and sometimes it is not. I rarely get angry."

Coming to age involves knowing what can and cannot be expected from others and from institutions. During my own midlife, I spent a lot of energy being angry with an organized religion that I felt was inadequate and almost totally unresponsive to my need to make sense of my spiritual experience. I felt I had given much to my institutional church over the years, and I had developed expectations of them. One evening, after I had given a presentation to a group of church members gathered at a retreat center, a wise woman in her late eighties who had been one of my former instructors called me aside. "How are you getting along with the church?" she asked. "Not much better than several years ago," I admitted. She hesitated a moment and then, with a twinkle in her eye, said, "Well, you know, we can't expect much of them, can we?" Before I

> *Coming to age involves knowing what can and cannot be expected from others and from institutions.*

could respond, she rose to go to bed. This woman remained a spiritual teacher, still pointing the way for others—and, I would suspect, still not expecting much from them—until her death a few years ago. "Not expecting much" is not about complacency, and it is not about cynicism. It is about knowing and accepting the limitations of others and of institutions, and knowing what we need to do for ourselves.

Yet many people coming to age, whether or not they are associated with organized religious institutions, do have a very sure, if inexpressible, sense that their lives are connected to Something Greater, and they are very careful not to limit It. As one wise person turning seventy said, "Truth is like a crystal with many facets, and we come to it through our own facet."

Jung calls this ultimate Truth the Infinite; the Sufis call it the Guest; some people speak of it as Love, Spirit, or Mystery; and many call it God—or sometimes Goddess. Personal experience, it seems, brings confidence of that connection to many in a direct, even mystical sense: "Without a shadow of a doubt, I felt His Presence," one woman said. "I was reading scripture and it was as though the passage was in red letters," said a man seeking direction. "My dream shed the light that my mind could not find," reported a woman. Others speak of a connection to Something Greater because it makes sense to them, although it still remains a mystery. "There must be a Plan," is the way this is often expressed, or "I'm a small part of a large body of Spirit." Many people talked of synchronistic events, which one person described as "God working autonomously," that provided a sense of connection for them. "I guess I would say that God opened and closed the doors," or "I don't talk much about it, but Someone has been looking after me my whole life," were typical comments.

Some people speak of feeling connected to nature, to the continuity of generations, and to creativity and creative expression. One woman, who calls herself an existentialist, gave these words to her experience: "Music is bigger than you are, bigger than I am, bigger than Mozart himself. Music comes from God."

The people who were interviewed were not chosen on the basis of any religious or nonreligious affiliation, and their beliefs represent a variety of approaches, including humanism and existentialism. Yet they did share one thing: Almost none felt he or she had answers about spiritual matters for others, although many have deeply satisfying personal faith. As one woman summarized her feelings: "The way I see it, God is spoken in many tongues, and the right way to speak may be still to be discovered."

Perhaps discovering one's own personal right way to speak about God or about ultimate concerns is the most significant task of later life. I believe Jung is correct when he says that the regaining of a religious attitude that allows us to see our own personal lives as moving toward wholeness, as filled with meaning, and as related to others and to Something Greater is the psychological/spiritual task for the later years.

Many creative people coming to age have found, in looking back, that their lives do hold meaning and connection. These people joyfully speak of their lives, with all their inherent victories and their struggles. One woman calls this process seeing "the fruition of the long term."

CHAPTER 2

FRUITION OF
THE LONG TERM

So if we wish to die well, we must learn
how to live well.

—Dalai Lama, *The Tibetan Book of*
Living and Dying

$\mathcal{A}$ vital, thoughtful woman of seventy-two years sat across from me at a table laden with books. She sipped a cup of fragrant herbal tea, and then with growing passion began to talk about the fruition of the long term:

> My work is a piece of art. There is joy in seeing the fruition of the long term. My life has a rhythm. One day in 1980, I was introducing myself in a group. When it was my turn to introduce myself I said, "I'm an artist," and that surprised me. I was always held back by self-doubt and by thinking maybe I was just a doodler. My husband helped me see my work differently. He made a video of my paintings over the years. I can see now that my painting is a work. My family is a work. The last twenty years have been a work. This is the fruition of the long term. You can't see that when you're young.

DISCERNING THE PATTERN

The accumulation of years cannot guarantee a sense of fruition, but it can provide the opportunity for such. Many creative people coming to age are able to look at their life and see its patterns, claim its meanings, and give thanks for it. They are able to come to appreciate what they have accomplished and to be satisfied, even though they may not have accomplished everything they wished.

"Ripely and quietly we look and we see," said one person. As people have time to think and to be—something our culture almost always denies to the young—they can often see that choices that at one time seemed random or even whimsical now form a coherent, meaningful whole. Often they also speak of life as more than the sum of their choices, as dependent on more than their own efforts. "Things happened and they fit," said one person. "It was meant to be," or "I was guided," said others. "My life has had a direction, and I didn't set it by myself. I didn't even recognize the direction for half a century," articulated one woman. Often people call these events synchronistic—coincidences that are meaningful. "I call it synchronicity when just the right book comes into my hands at the right time," said one person.

And even though many people are quick to explain that not all the things that have happened to them have been of their doing, they still have a sense that they have lived a very particular life. The fruition of the long term is about the development of something uniquely one's own. One man expressed it well when he explained, "I feel good about my life for I know I have become a large percentage of that which I was put on Earth to become." Creative people coming to age know that the choices they have made mattered. "Because I say my life was guided does not mean I made no choices. In fact, I made significant choices, but the pattern was not *just* my own," said one woman. This, I believe, is what the master students of human nature have named *integrity* (Erikson), *individuation* (Jung), and *self-actualization* (Maslow).

The pattern that is discerned often contains darkness as well as light. Lives of creative people coming to age are peppered with pain, and they often realize they have caused pain for others. Yet we accept difficulties and limitations as the material for growth. This does not mean that people coming to age have no regrets. They do have regrets, and they often desire forgiveness. They often wish for less physical diminishment, yet they can usually find the strength to tolerate it. They talk about enduring difficult things. "We come to know that suffering doesn't come because we are good or bad or because we caused or failed to prevent it. Rather, we come to know that suffering comes because that is how life is," said one person. Sometimes the difficulties are seen as more than just something to be tolerated. Sometimes they are seen as "soul work." One woman talked of learning something through grief and depression that has supported her lifelong journey:

> My mother died when I was fifty, and since my father had died five years earlier, I was, at fifty, an orphan. *Orphan* was an important word. I knew I was orphaned, and I had feelings of shock and aloneness. I tried to deal with it. My automatic response was, as it had always been, to find a way within myself to deal with the loneliness and shock. It took a long time, and I did finally seek some help for depression. The best way I can describe the state I'm talking about is as a state of emptiness. It was as though I should fill the hole inside but I couldn't—and no matter how much I was part of a crowd or of a family, I was still alone. I came to know the meaning of the adage, We're born alone and we die alone. The emptiness that I couldn't fill was terrifying. One day I had a hallucination. I saw a desert, with dry trees on the horizon that I couldn't reach. I felt I was tumbling through space with nothing to hold on to. It was frightening. I think my body was saying "let go." Anyway, I was able to stay with these feelings, and it is interesting, I think, that staying with the terrifying feelings of emptiness has led to my sense of contentment. I don't have to fill the emptiness, and that is very freeing. It was reassuring to read about the Desert Fathers who had known what I had experienced. The desert has become a metaphor for me, a metaphor about not cluttering up my life.

Death, grief, depression, relationship breakups, job losses, faith disillusionments—all these can close doors and often feel as though they will break the heart, but they can be learning experiences as well. One person said, "I learned more about my own direction from the doors that closed behind me than from those that opened in front of me." It may be useless and unkind to talk to someone who is in the middle of a devastating sadness about how things eventually work out for the best. Yet many people coming to age find that things do eventually work out. One woman, paraphrasing *Romans* 8:28, said, "All things work together for good. This passage has to do with people who live truthfully with love. As the Zen Buddhists know, everything is as it should be and everything is changing."

This sense that things are as they are supposed to be and that our lives have a sense of fruition helps answer our need for meaning and helps us prepare, when the time is right, to finally let life go. The sense of meaning and of acceptance protects us from despair. Erik Erikson, American psychologist and life-stage theorist, knew this when he chose the words *wisdom* and *integrity* to symbolize the strength of the last stage of the life cycle. Erikson, his wife, Joan, and Helen Kivnick explain what they mean by wisdom as the symbol of the last stage of life:

> We have elected wisdom as the word that symbolizes the strength of the last stage of the life cycle and have used the words integrity and despair to represent the opposing poles that characterize the tension in the psyche. Integrity we chose because it seems to describe the aging individual's struggles to integrate the strength and purpose necessary to maintain wholeness despite disintegrating physical capacities. It also suggests the need to gather the experiences of a long and eventful life into a meaningful pattern. . . . In the same way, elements of despair have inevitably been ingredients of every struggle. . . . To have experienced this world and our human inadequacy to deal with one another and our mutual problems in living and growing is consistently to know defeat. . . . Some of these components may be isolated and defined but the genuinely wise have in some way managed to integrate them all. The oldest and wisest elders understand that situations are complex and that many factors have to be weighed and distinguished. (1986, p. 288)

Meaning, purpose, and fulfillment may come from realizing that our lives and our development were never for ourselves alone.

The fruition of the long term may be even more than wisdom or individuation or self-actualization. It may be more than seeing our lives as having patterns and being filled with meaningful events. Meaning, purpose, and fulfillment may come from realizing that our lives and our development were never for ourselves alone. Instead of being narcissistic and selfish, we may come to see that attention to our own development has benefited those around us and the universe as well. In fact, we can come to know that human development is the only thing that can move society ahead—and perhaps even save it from destruction. We may see that our lives are connected to something other than ourselves and cannot be wiped out even by personal diminishments and death. Speaking of this realization that our lives are larger than our personal histories, Jung (1965) says:

> The decisive question for man [woman] is: Is he [she] related to something infinite or not? That is the telling question of his [her] life. Only if we know that the thing which truly matters is the infinite can we avoid fixing our interest upon futilities, and upon all kinds of goals which are not of real importance. (p. 325)

ENGAGING IN THE SEARCH

In midlife, people tend to be caught in the world, in their strivings, their fears, their regrets. They agonize over their choices—the wrong ones they have made and the possibility of wrong ones they may make. They rave at individuals and institutions whom they have expected to fulfill their needs and whom they find unable or unwilling to do so. They spend time and energy trying to discover or remake relationships with people, work, and belief systems they hope will satisfy them and fill them up.

But in midlife people are also invited —if they are lucky and if they can embrace life and not hold back—to experience something more. They are invited to enter the search for that which can lead them home—right through their

> *People see the patterns of their life, its meaning, and the fruition of their efforts, and they do not have to cling to the past.*

sixties and seventies and beyond. They must take their journeys in whatever way they are called to them. Journeys may take different forms for different people. They must engage in the search, for the search is the way. There are certainly ways to defend against this search, to defend against life for that matter, but refusing to engage in the search does not serve the later years well. Most aware, creative people who are beyond midlife have found a way to live that brings them satisfaction, and it is almost never a mere replay of their earlier life. Their later years are related to their earlier years, but they go beyond them. People see the patterns of their life, its meaning, and the fruition of their efforts, and they do not have to cling to the past. They have a sense of meaning and of fruition, and they are freed by this.

Some people, regardless of their age, are reluctant to change or to journey. We can understand the reluctance to engage in the search—or to engage in life, for that matter—but we must also understand the cost of refusal. People living with consciousness and intentionality in their later life have, almost without exception, engaged in the search in their own ways, either consciously or unconsciously. We know this to be true, for we see the fruits of it. Their lives are not just repeat performances of earlier life. The tasks of those coming to age are different from those they addressed in the heat of the middle years.

Helen Luke (1987, pp. 28–29) speaks of the occupations of the old. She defines the work of those consciously aging as prayer, spontaneous joy, and the passing on of wisdom. Prayer is not the saying of any pre-scribed set of words, but rather an attention to life. Luke notes one other task for those growing old gracefully. She sees the occupation of age as lis-tening, truly listening, to those still caught in power. One woman of nine-ty, confined to her bed and unable to feed or clothe herself, said with a wis-dom reserved for the old, "There is little I can do, but I can pray. I can pray for all those younger people who are too busy to pray for themselves."

The fruition of the long term is about coming to age with aware-ness, with grace, and with great care for one's living. Quaker author Mary Morrison (1994) speaks of this stage of life:

> We have had our world as in our time; and if we re-live it well in memo-ry, it will bring us its wisdom. We will see our life, each of us, as the whole that it is. Events that seemed random will be seen as parts of a coherent whole. Decisions that we were hardly aware of making will reveal them-selves as significant choices; and we can honestly and dispassionately repent the poor ones and rejoice in the good ones. We can call up emo-tions that seemed devastating in their time, and recollect them in tran-quility, forgiving others and ourselves. When we do this we have truly had our world in our time, and it is in our possession from that time on. Now we look with new eyes at the present, and at the younger ones who are having the world in their time. If our hearts are in the right place, if we have done our harvesting well, we can look at them and love them in their passage through the stages that we remember well, but are now seeing from a different perspective as beautiful parts of a whole that we could not see while we were living it. (p. 12)

THE LEAVING

It seems that having had the world in our time, as Morrison described, is precisely what allows us to be able to leave it willingly. Creative people coming to age acknowledge the beauty of their time and their gratitude for it, as did one eighty-four-year-old retired school principal: "Life is like a good book. You hate to see it come to an end, but you couldn't enjoy it if it didn't have an end. Things come together. Life has been good to me. I've been lucky."

It was interesting during the interview process for this book to notice the difference between the way midlife people and older people speak of the end of life. Midlife people are often aware for the first time that life is limited, and they may feel tremendous pressure in light of this awareness. They speak a great deal about death, although their death is probably quite distant. Pressure to find a life mission, to make life changes in order to get more in line with that mission, and not to make a mistake or

> *Older people, who in actuality are much closer to the end of life, usually express much less concern about it.*

waste precious time marks the midlife attitude about death. Older people, who in actuality are much closer to the end of life, usually express much less concern about it. They seem, allowing for some denial and some resignation that are often present around this subject, quite accepting of death—though not always of the process of dying.

With each interview, besides listening for a sense of the fruition of life, I asked for reflection on the final letting go—on death and dying. I did this because I feel that developing a sense of having lived well and making preparation for leaving life are the central issues of the later years. There are certainly other issues: It is important that people have sufficient income, health care, respect, and safe and loving places to live. Many people spoke of these issues, and of the political and economic factors involved in providing for a more comfortable retirement. It is important that we be involved with these issues, but it is also important that we not get caught up in them, for social and economic well-being alone cannot finally bring satisfaction to those aging consciously nor bring peace to the departing soul.

So I asked people about their lives as works of art and about their thoughts on their death and dying. A few did not respond to my inquiry about death and I dropped the subject, but most of the people interviewed did desire to share their thoughts. Concern focused much more on the process of dying than on death itself. Almost without exception, people talked about their desire not to be a burden to others, and about their desire for the process of death not to be lingering, painful, or incapacitating. There was grief for "what time has stolen" along with an appreciation of the moments left. As the time for death draws nearer, fears revolve around being alone, uncared for, or a body out of control. Although bodily diminishments may be seen as an opportunity for soul making, they are rarely welcomed and often raged against. Many people seem to agree with Florida Scott-Maxwell (1968), who wrote: "My only fear about death is that it will not come soon enough. Life still interests and occupies me . . . but please God I die before I lose my independence" (p. 75).

The responses to my questions about death were as varied as the responses to other topics. Almost without exception these creative people coming to age reported that they had come to some acceptance of death, although some didn't think there was anything really worth saying about that. "It just is." A few others passed off the subject with lighthearted responses, perhaps as a means of denial or perhaps because this is "just another silly unanswerable question." One woman contemplated her fear that, if we die as we live, which she believes to be true, she will not be able to let go easily since tenacity marked her life. Some found comfort and solace in their religious belief systems. Some felt able to trust the Power that had been present for them in life to be present in death. Such comments as " It will be a glorious banquet in the sky," and "I'll go where He has prepared a place for me," and "It will be the last and greatest adventure" were offered.

In the discussion of our own death, all of us are equal, not one of us having experienced death personally. But most of the creative people coming to age seemed able to walk toward this ultimate letting go without undue concern. Perhaps it is an attitude they share, such as this reflection by Mary Morrison (1994): "Maybe the general truth is that *any* process, not held back from, is fulfilling and beautiful. I hope I can remember that when I'm dying" (p. 23). Or perhaps it is confidence that these people share, such as that expressed by one woman I interviewed: "He'll give you the ticket when you're ready to get on the train."

CHAPTER 3

THE LENS OF JUNGIAN PSYCHOLOGY

In the morning it [the sun] rises from the nocturnal sea of unconsciousness and looks upon the wide, bright world. . . . At the stroke of noon the descent begins. And the descent means the reversal of all the ideals and values that were cherished in the morning.

—C. G. Jung, *Stages of Life*

$\mathcal{M}$any theorists have contributed to our understanding of adult development by looking at aging, life stages, and transitions. Individuals including Erik Erikson, Roger Gould, Daniel Levinson, and Gail Sheehy have provided an abundance of data on chronological stages. Abraham Maslow's hierarchy of needs theory has greatly enlightened our understanding of the developmental nature of needs. Bernice Neugarten, along with some other adult development theorists, stresses the importance of context in understanding personality aging. And gerontologist Robert Havinghurst, among others, proposes continued activity for aging people.

41

Most theorists recognize that early life requires the establishment of self-identity, along with the ability for some intimacy and some sense of agency, or ability to make things happen. They also usually recognize that later life requires more emphasis on personal authenticity, completeness, and concern for future generations. The theorists differ in the importance they place on the need for interiority and the importance of social context. They vary in their emphasis on the importance of spirituality and of midlife as a transition period. Many theorists view midlife as a period when people recognize that time is running out, that loss is a part of life, and that roles and relationships must change if life is not to become stagnant. Jung agrees with this, but places an even more profound emphasis on midlife, seeing the midlife purpose as the deep reorienting of personality and the pursuing of soul work.

Some of the key ideas of several adult developmental stage theorists are presented in the chart on page 43.

THE JUNGIAN LIFE STAGE THEORY

Carl Gustav Jung has been called the father of adult development. His ideas emphasize interiority, wholeness, and a search for meaning as primary tasks for aging people. His life stage theory, which emphasizes the categories of childhood, youth, middle age, and old age, is particularly instructive when combined with his psychological type theory. By identifying age-related and personality-related patterns, the Jungian model allows us to suggest certain characteristics of different life stages and to observe how these stage-related themes might be experienced by people with different personality structures.

The Jungian model suggests certain characteristics of different life stages.

In the Jungian model, each stage of life has its own developmental requirements. These requirements, while generally universal, have specific coloration influenced by the personality structure of the person experiencing them. Jungian theory is sometimes criticized for its emphasis on the individual, particularly its emphasis on interior development as opposed to interrelational dynamics. Some criticize its neglect of social issues such as adequate housing, health care, financial security, and other important matters. There certainly is an emphasis on the psyche in Jungian psychology, but there is also a recognition of the importance of

STAGES OF ADULTHOOD

	As Conceptualized by Gould, Levinson, Erikson, and Sheehy	As Conceptualized by Jung
Early Adulthood *Early Stages*	• Can feel provisional and tentative • Issues of identity and intimacy emerge • Tentative commitments to careers, relationships, and lifestyle important	• Adaptation and accommodation to the outer world
Later Stages	• Can feel more settled and stable • Issues revolve around commitment and achievement in work, family, community • Development of the dream important • Acquisition of a mentor may occur • Emphasis is on "shoulds" and on the importance of willpower	• Specialization • Achievement • Development of ego and persona important
Midlife	• Can feel disorienting, confusing, and lonely • Issues revolve around loss, time running out, autonomy, and personal authenticity • Recognition of differences between the dream and reality occurs • Needs arise for role changes and recognition of neglected parts of self	• Reversal of psychic energy from outer direction to inner, from accommodation to completion • Sense of loss and need to integrate nondeveloped parts of personality (including Shadow) • Spiritual crisis as ego and persona are seen as inadequate • Search for meaning

	As Conceptualized by Erikson, Gould, Levinson, and Sheehy	As Conceptualized by Jung
Late Adulthood *Early Stages*	• Can feel calmer, more settled, generative, productive, renewed	
	• Issue of living and working defined more by one's authentic self and less by outer forces	• Focus on inner life—movement toward integration of all parts of Self as ego relinquishes total control to allow emergence of the Self as Center of Personality
	• Emphasis on relationship, lifestyle, and role changes	
Later Stages	• Can feel integrated, more accepting, more "at one with the universe"	• Movement toward recognition of one's unique mission and meaning and one's connection to all others and to the Source of the Self
	• Issues emerge involving retirement, finances, health and lifestyle, life's meaning, relationship to future generations, limitations, and loss of faculties	

bringing to the world what has been learned on one's personal journey. As has often been said, Jungian psychology is about transforming the world "from the inside out." From this viewpoint, society is transformed and renewed to the extent that *individuals* are transformed and renewed. The model recognizes that context is important, but it contends that personal development, or *individuation,* can take place in spite of difficulties such as bodily diminishment, poverty, lack of societal supports, emotional deprivations, and a host of other difficulties. In fact it is often in the midst of the greatest distress that quantum leaps in consciousness are made. History has shown that it is often creative people in the most disruptive of circumstances who, by their own development, have helped move the world forward. A contemporary example of this is Vaclav Havel, playwright and creative president of the Czech Republic, who frequently speaks of the salvation of the world lying in the human heart.

JUNG'S LIFE STAGES MODEL

First Half of Life	**Midlife Transition**	**Second Half of Life**
Accommodation	*Reevaluation*	*Reintegration*
• Energy directed primarily toward outer world	• Energy directed primarily toward inner world	• Energy can flow between inner and outer worlds
• Feelings of striving and engaging in life	• Feelings of tension between need for personal time and space and the heavy responsibilities and demands from others	• Feelings of spontaneity, purpose, acceptance
• Meaning found in meeting biological and survival needs (reproducing, achieving in career, establishing homes/relationships, building self-confidence, and so on)	• Meaning found in spiritual reassessment; meeting biological and survival needs begins to fail to satisfy	• Meaning found in movement toward wholeness (i.e., connection of conscious and unconscious, of ego and Self) and in contributing from this place of wholeness to spiritual and cultural development of society
• Requires differentiation and specialization	• Requires recognition of feelings of loss, incompleteness (i.e., missing parts of self)	• Requires some integration of all parts of Self
• Concentration on developing persona and ego	• Shadow emergence	• Contrasexual parts of Self emerge

Jung (1981) suggests in his stage of life essay a model that delineates four life stages: childhood, youth, middle age, and old age. We who use Jung's model often collapse it into what we call first half of life, second half of life, and the midlife transition that serves as the bridge between the two. The chart above, which Katharine Myers, Eleanor Corlett, and I developed for our midlife workshops, identifies some of the characteristics of these stages. For a type-specific overview of the stages, see the chart on pages 154–155 of this book.

In this model, the first half of life is seen as a period of ego development and accommodation (adaptation). It is the period in which we come to have some sense of who we are. This sense of identity is often developed as young people accommodate or adapt themselves to their environments in order to find their work, form relationships and families, and discover or carve out a place for themselves in the social order. This ego work is necessary for success in the world and for encouraging a sense of identity and self-worth. But this accommodation to culture also can lead to the development of what has been called a *false self*—one that pleases others and gains respect and rewards at the expense of its own essence. In other words, although concentrating on developing the ego can bring status and acceptance and can lead to various important achievements, it also can lead to one-sided development that is directed toward adapting to society in order to receive its rewards and blessings at the expense of developing one's true self. Jung (1981) writes: "We overlook the essential fact that the social goal is attained only at the cost of the diminution of personality" (par. 772).

Midlife is often a time of reevaluation when the life that has been directed toward looking to authority figures and to others in society for direction rather than looking to oneself often comes to feel unreliable, at best. It is a time when those parts of our selves that have been repressed in the service of adaptation or that have not yet been developed often call for inclusion. It is the time when people ask, Is this all there is? Those things that we have not yet developed in ourselves and in our lives may be demanding integration into the personality and the life of the midlife person. This is a time of turmoil, a time when the ego struggles to hold on to its primacy and its sense of security while being battered by relatively unknown forces that also want a place at the psyche's table. The very fact that life may seem constricted and tight at midlife can have meaning. It can announce the need for expansion.

The turmoil experienced in the middle passage can last a long time. Midlife transition is meant to lead to the death of some things and the birth of others, and it can be a trying and lengthy process. It will last until a new equilibrium is established between who we were and who we are to be, or until we tire and relapse into old patterns that we are afraid to relinquish. If the transition is successful, people will emerge from it with an expanded sense of who they are—they may be more flexible, spontaneous, and compassionate and may have a deeper sense of purpose and connection. When the transition is not successful, people may spend their later years holding desperately to outlived patterns and ideas and may be seen by others as rigid, controlling, and outdated.

Although the turmoil of the midlife period may seem endless, it does come to an end. This shift usually occurs when people reintegrate those attitudes, activities, and parts of themselves that, although always present, were denied expression in earlier life. The shift occurs when they learn to look within themselves for a sense of authority and when those parts of personality and life that have been excluded are included, at least to some extent. It is important to remember that the previously unrecognized aspects of ourselves

In the later stages of life, it may be even more important to know that we are living connected to our true selves.

and our lives are to be *integrated*—not capitulated to. The purpose of those undeveloped aspects is not to dominate the personality—people do remain basically who they were—but rather to enter the personality, expand it, and make it more flexible, open, and compassionate. This process of expansion brings the recognition that life is more than one's conscious ego, more than what one knows about oneself. It can bring recognition that life has implications that are more than personal and that can lead to new commitments and vision for the next stage of life as one sees more clearly one's place in the larger scheme of things. The outer life begins to match the inner knowledge, and sometimes this newfound and truly authentic power allows creative people coming to age to transform the environments they inhabit.

As people age, many things that we call *ego concerns* continue to seem important, and in fact they are. It matters greatly that people have adequate income and appropriate housing, that they have a sense of security and preserve their health. But although all these things matter, they cannot of themselves satisfy. In the later stages of life, it may be even more important to know that we are living connected to our true selves and are comfortable knowing our place in the universe. The involvements that bring meaning in early life and those that bring meaning in later life are not the same, as Jung (1981) writes:

> A human being would certainly not grow to be seventy or eighty years old if this longevity had no meaning for the species. The afternoon of human life must also have a significance of its own and cannot be merely a pitiful appendage to life's morning. The significance of the morning undoubtedly lies in the individual, our entrenchment in the outer world, the propagation of our kind, and the care of our children. This is the obvious purpose of

nature. But when this purpose has been attained—and more than attained—shall the earning of money, the extension of conquests, and the expansion of life go steadily on beyond the bounds of all reason and sense? Whoever carries over into the afternoon the law of the morning, or the natural aim, must pay for it with damage to his soul, just as surely as a growing youth who tries to carry over his childish egotism into adult life must pay for this mistake with social failure. Money-making, social achievement, family and posterity are nothing but plain nature, not culture. Culture lies outside the purpose of nature. Could by any chance culture be the meaning and purpose of the second half of life? (par. 787)

It seems that we *must* live this drama. It appears we are born to it. We come into this world with all our personality *in potentia,* but it takes a lifetime of living to bring that which is potential into reality. Another way of saying this is that we are born whole, born as we are to be; but we must spend our lives becoming what we already are.

Since we have a finite amount of psychic energy, we tend as young people to develop those parts of ourselves that are most natural to us and/or that allow us to adapt to our environments. Ideally this kind of development helps us have a sense of who we are and allows others to interact with us. Yet at midlife, those parts of ourselves that we have not developed may cry out for recognition. For example, if we have developed our ability to nurture others at the expense of our ability to nurture ourselves, we may at midlife have to learn to care for ourselves as well. Jung (1981) says that at midlife, "many—far too many—aspects of life which should also have been experienced lie in the lumber room among dusty memories; but sometimes there are glowing coals under gray ashes" (par. 772).

It is difficult to get through the gray ashes to the glowing coals. James Hollis (1995), Jungian analyst and author, tells us that the only way we can judge ourselves or others is by examining how well we have been able to become ourselves in spite of those things that would hold us back. Those things that would hold us back are often the parts of ourselves that lie in the lumber room among the dusty memories. Those parts of ourselves want to live in reality as well as *in potentia.* They want to expand us, to teach us about breadth and depth. And because undeveloped parts of ourselves usually come to us in primitive form—in fact often making us look rather foolish—they can teach us a great deal about humility, vulnerability, and compassion as well.

The life development stages presented here can serve us by giving us a model, although, as with all models, they may be inadequate when applied to any particular life. In addition, Jung's theory of type and now type development theory—as articulated by such people as Isabel Myers, Harold Grant, and, more recently, Katharine Myers, Linda Kirby, Nancy Barger, and Naomi Quenk—make the life stages concept relate more specifically to individual development. Type theory can help us understand ourselves and others, and type development theory can serve as a practical guide to vital, conscious aging. Using these concepts can help us move closer to being that which we were created to be—that which we hold *in potentia*—and identify issues that might hold us back.

JUNGIAN TYPE THEORY

Jungian type theory offers a way of viewing personality. It suggests that people have a preferred way of orienting themselves toward and being in the world. It suggests that people prefer to interact primarily with either the outer environment that surrounds them or with the inner world that they know inside themselves. It also suggests two primary mental functions: the *perceiving function,* which influences how we prefer to perceive or acquire information, and the *judging function,* which influences how we prefer to make decisions.

According to the theory, some people prefer to orient themselves primarily toward the outer world. These people are at home when interacting with the outer world of objects, people, and events. Their focus is broad and is on activity and interaction with others. Other people more naturally orient themselves toward their inner worlds. They are at home when they are processing their own experiences, thoughts, and feelings. Their focus is more in-depth, and they require time and space for introspection.

All people have a primary method for acquiring information. Some people prefer to perceive through their senses. These people take in information mainly through the five senses and recognize and trust what they can see, feel, touch, hear, taste, or otherwise experience directly. Others prefer to perceive primarily through their intuition. They generally take in information through their imaginations, recognizing and trusting hunches, inspirations, fantasies, and patterns that emerge.

Everyone has a predominant way of making decisions with the information they take in. Some people prefer to make their decisions primarily through their value systems. They tend to make choices as their hearts decide, based on what seems right or good or pleasing. Other individuals prefer instead to make decisions through their thinking function. They tend to make choices as their heads dictate, based on logic and analysis.

The *Myers-Briggs Type Indicator*® (MBTI) personality inventory is based on Jung's theory of personality and measures individual preferences for ways of being in the world. People who prefer to orient themselves toward the outer world are called *Extraverts,* and those who more naturally orient themselves toward the inner world are referred to as *Introverts.* People who perceive through their senses are called *Sensing types,* and those who prefer to perceive through their intuition are called *Intuitive types.* People who make their decisions primarily through their value systems are referred to as *Feeling types,* and those who more naturally make their decisions through their thinking function are referred to as *Thinking types.*

Isabel Myers contributed to psychological type theory by adding a fourth dimension to the MBTI, which was implied in Jung's theory. This is the Judging–Perceiving dimension, and it points toward lifestyle issues. People who prefer the Perceiving attitude tend to live lives marked by flexibility, spontaneity, and open-endedness. People who prefer the Judging attitude tend to live lives marked by order, closure, and planfulness. The Judging–Perceiving dimension also leads to the ordering of the functions, that is, the identification of the dominant, auxiliary, tertiary, and inferior functions. This ordering, which will be discussed later in this chapter, is important as a guide for exploring type development, and it is particularly essential to thinking about how our type develops and how we change in the second half of life.

In early life we tend to orient ourselves toward either the outer world or the inner world, to develop the mental functions we prefer, and to develop a preference for a lifestyle attitude. These preferences are the basis for our four-letter MBTI type code. Some examples of different type codes are described in the following paragraphs.

Suzanne's psychic energy flows primarily toward the outer world. This means that she is primarily energized by interactions with other people, with events, and with external stimuli of all kinds. We would say that she has an Extraverted (E) preference. The psychic energy of her Introverted (I) friend Joel is primarily directed toward his inner world, where he is energized by silence, time alone, and the inner drama that plays out "behind his forehead."

Preferring to perceive through her imagination and bursts of insight, Suzanne sees many connections and possibilities and trusts things that she cannot directly know through her senses. We would say that she is an Intuitive (N) type, unlike her Sensing (S) friend Joel, who prefers to perceive primarily through his senses and recognizes the reality of situations and trusts things he has witnessed or experienced.

Suzanne's decision-making process relies primarily on her value system (her heart) for guidance. We would say that she has a Feeling (F) preference in choice making, as opposed to a Thinking (T) preference like Joel, who, when faced with a decision, completes a cognitive and logical analysis of the data at hand.

Suzanne and Joel also adopt a dominant style for meeting their worlds. Suzanne prefers a planned, structured, decisive way of dealing with life, which marks a preference for Judging (J). Joel would rather follow a spontaneous, flexible, go-with-the-flow way of dealing with life, characteristic of a Perceiving (P) preference.

Looking at all of these preferences, we would say that Suzanne prefers Extraversion, Intuition, Feeling, and Judging. Her MBTI type code would be ENFJ. Joel prefers Introversion, Sensing, Thinking, and Perceiving, and his MBTI type code is ISTP.

There are sixteen possible MBTI type codes, and each type code is determined by the combination of letters abbreviating the person's preferences. For descriptions of the sixteen types, refer to appendix A. For a more complete explanation of type theory, you might wish to consult *Introduction to Type®* (Myers, 1993).

With the information provided by Suzanne's and Joel's type codes, we know some (but certainly not all) of the important things about them. We know something of the ways they prefer to be in the world. The letters of their type codes represent their preferences, but they also have some capacity for the preferences represented by the letters that are not in their type codes. They were each born with their whole personality—all the type attitudes and

> *The letters of our type code represent our preferences, but we also have some capacity for the preferences represented by the letters that are not in our type code.*

functions—*in potentia.* The recognition of, relationship to, and maybe even the true development of those preferences *in potentia* can lead to more complete personality. This work is often reserved for the second half of life.

TYPE DEVELOPMENT THEORY

As we have said, the development of our type preferences (denoted by the four-letter type codes we have been describing) gives a person a sense of self and of a consistent personality that others can relate to. Ideally, this development assists one in the securing of a place in society and in forming meaningful relationships and work that will reinforce the person's sense of self, a primary psychological task of the first half of life.

Suzanne has the potential not only for developing her preferences for Extraversion, Intuition, Feeling, and Judging, but also for developing her capacity for Introversion, Sensing, Thinking, and Perceiving. Likewise, Joel will develop some level of Extraversion, Intuition, Feeling, and Judging capacity, even though his preferences are for Introversion, Sensing, Thinking, and Perceiving. It is often around the middle of life when the unchosen, and probably underdeveloped, type preferences begin to demand inclusion in personality. It may take Suzanne, Joel, and all of us an entire lifetime to realize our type development potential, since the psyche seems to have a finite amount of psychic energy and does not seem capable of developing all functions simultaneously.

Type development theory proposes that, ideally, people will first develop the type preferences with which they are most comfortable. They will develop their most preferred mental function (either the perceiving function of Intuition or Sensing or the judging function of Thinking or Feeling) in their preferred attitude (Extraverted or Introverted) early in their lives. This is referred to in psychological type theory as the *dominant function*. They will then develop their other mental function in the opposite attitude to assist them—called the *auxiliary function*.

For example, Suzanne, because she is an ENFJ, ideally will develop her dominant Feeling function at a young age and direct it toward the outer world. This will give her some ability to make decisions and to relate to the outer world. She will then develop her auxiliary perceiving function, which is Intuition, in order to have a way of gathering data for her decision making, and she will direct this toward her inner world. With all this first-half-of-life work, Suzanne will have a preferred orientation toward the outer world but also some access to her inner world. She will also have a preferred way of acquiring information and of making decisions. Since her dominant function (Feeling) is a judging function, she will appear orderly, decisive, and planful. For information on the developmental sequence of functions for the sixteen types, refer to appendix B. For a complete explanation of the theory of type development you might wish to consult *Introduction to Type®️ Dynamics and Development* (Myers and Kirby, 1994).

We have assumed that Suzanne lives in a an environment that has allowed her development to follow her natural pattern. Assuming this, her second-half-of-life type development task will be to make acquaintance with her nonpreferred functions. These functions are called *tertiary* and *inferior* in the language of typology. This process will enrich her life and assist her in being more nearly the complete, whole person she was created to be.

The development progression outlined for Suzanne is an ideal. In actuality, type development progresses for people in an individual way. People can get derailed from their natural type development patterns. If one's natural preferences are not supported, one often adapts and leaves parts of oneself, some of one's type preferences, in the

If one's natural preferences are not supported, one often lives an adapted or false type.

lumber room. In other words, one lives an adapted or false type. And those undeveloped aspects of self, those undeveloped type preferences, become Jung's "glowing embers under gray ashes." They tend to make themselves known around the middle years when less energy is available to act a part not one's own.

Consider Eduardo (ENFP), raised by his single mother and educated primarily through his own efforts. Eduardo's story illustrates how we often come to live out of some of our nonpreferred type preferences in our early lives, particularly in our work. Before his retirement, Eduardo spent his days working as an accountant for a small CPA firm. A large percentage of each day was spent in a manner contrary to his natural preferences: working alone (Introversion), on a strict schedule (Judging), and making detailed calculations that followed prescribed procedures (Sensing), he also missed having camaraderie with and receiving affirmation from clients and co-workers (Feeling). Eduardo liked his clients and occasionally spoke with them, but most of the time he felt isolated, confined, and quite often bored as well. Eduardo acted—in his work, at least—like an ISTJ. Now, in retirement, he feels that he has come home to himself. He experiences great delight in the spontaneity of his life

(Perceiving) and in the opportunity he now has to interact with a large number of friends and acquaintances (Extraversion). He is taking painting classes, volunteering in a Big Brothers program, traveling with his close group of men friends who are also retired, and writing a bit of poetry—all activities in line with his Intuition and Feeling preferences. He is now, in retirement, honoring his preferred type letters and feels at home with them, but he is grateful for having learned some skill with his nonpreferred functions in his work.

Even if culture has been supportive, type development has gone well, and people feel they have been living out of their true type, there is still type development work that is reserved for the later part of life. There are undeveloped pieces of ourselves, our nonpreferred type functions, that we have had neither the time nor the opportunity to develop in our earlier years.

For example, Jenlyn (ISFJ) is a wife, a mother, and a teacher in an elementary school. She feels, unlike Eduardo, that her early life allowed her to live out of her type preferences, at least most of the time: Her classes were small, and her family and home allowed for a great deal of intimacy and "down time" (Introversion). She was secure in her knowledge of her work tasks (Sensing), and she felt appreciated by both her students and her family (Feeling). She also felt she usually had a sense of control over her ordered life (Judging). Jenlyn describes her early life as contented most of the time, but in her forties, she found herself, quite unexpectedly, experiencing the call to development.

Jenlyn began having recurring dreams in which she found herself drawn toward a group of people whom she perceived as being very different from anyone she had known previously. These new people were interested in myriad things she didn't know about. She found them very stimulating, yet sometimes they tired her. She loved their sense of playfulness, even though she was not certain that she could trust them or relax in their presence. She admired their ability to articulate their reasons for doing the things they did, and even to debate with each other, but she felt inferior and intimidated by them.

Jenlyn did not feel that she was returning home in the sense that Eduardo did. In her middle years she was being called to develop some parts of herself that she felt somewhat uncomfortable with, but that could enrich her life and bring her closer to her potential wholeness. She, too, had glowing coals under gray ashes—type preferences waiting for the proper time to announce themselves. As she, in her fifties and sixties, has developed her own wider vision (Intuition), her own confidence in presenting her personal positions (Thinking), and her own sense of playfulness (Perceiving), she has found herself stimulated and energized, if sometimes "stretched" as well.

We all have parts of ourselves that we have neglected. As someone suggested, everyone has had to drop some things in the mad rush to catch the bus. Most people drop some aspects of themselves in their mad rush to earn a living, manage a home, raise children, and attend to the needs of their community. Reconnecting with an interest from childhood can sometimes help those in midlife and beyond renew their lives as well as offer to those around them something that is uniquely theirs to offer.

Both of the scenarios outlined here—the rediscovering of aspects of oneself that have been dropped, and developing nonpreferred aspects of the self that have not yet had the opportunity to be developed—can begin in the middle years and pay dividends in later life. To those who, like Eduardo, have been adapting and living out of some nonpreferred type letter(s) the emergence of undeveloped preferences often feels like coming home. These people realize they have been walking sideways and find it less stressful to walk straight in their own paths. To those who, like Jenlyn, have been living primarily out of their preferred type preferences, the emergence of the nonpreferred type preferences feels foreign. They sense that incorporating them will be difficult, though perhaps exciting and life renewing as well.

In either case, this emergence can pave the way for the coming to age period, in which we can live more fully out of our natural type preferences and relate in some ways to those type preferences that are not our own. Some development of our nondeveloped preferences can help us become more completely ourselves.

If, as Jung suggests, meaning in later life comes from movement toward becoming the whole people we were created to be, is it possible that type development can be a guiding light? Is it possible that type development can help us incorporate, in the service of wholeness, those parts of ourselves that we have not yet developed? Is it possible

If life is a journey toward wholeness, is it possible that type development can light the way?

that in this process we find joy, spontaneity, and adventure, and that we learn humility and creativity? Can more conscious and complete type development help us find a sense of connection with and compassion toward others? Is this a necessary step toward the awareness that our individual lives are, in fact, more than we consciously know—that they are infused with energy that can trigger the evolution of our own stories and, perhaps, the Greater Story as well? Part 2 will address the following questions:

- How do people age creatively?
- Are there identifiable themes that indicate movement toward creative aging?
- What are the commonalities and differences among people aging creatively?
- What does it mean to become oneself in the face of what holds one back?
- Do elders who live life with zest, creativity, and compassion feel in touch with any Force greater than themselves? If so, how do they describe this experience?

As we explore these questions, I will share my observations from years of experience and from recent investigation. I will use a general framework of psychological type theory to deepen the understanding of my observations. And, finally, I will share with you the stories of more than fifty creative people who are coming to age with grace and wisdom and who can articulate their experiences for us. I ask you to listen to these stories without expecting formulas or imposed consistency. Let yourself experience their stories, and you will hear.

Life has changed me greatly, it has

improved me greatly, but it has also

left me practically the same.

—Florida Scott-Maxwell,

Measure of My Days

PART 2

UNEXPECTED JOYS OF THE LATER YEARS

*M*ost creatively aging people will agree that life has changed them, even improved them, in many ways; but in many ways it has also left them the same. The fact that "leopards do not change their spots" was brought to my attention more than once while gathering data for this book. Yet we must also recognize, as Jung did, that if people do not change as they age, they may become rigid caricatures of their earlier selves. The descriptive words of Jung (1981) for those who remain unchanged—"hypochondriacs, niggards, pedants, applauders of the past or else eternal adolescents" (par. 785)—may ring a bit too true to our ears. Unfortunately, we often see all around us what life looks like when the second act is simply a rerun of the first. When creative people coming to age face and meet the challenges of this time, they find that there are unexpected joys and special gifts that have been reserved for the later years.

On the archetypal heroic journey, the journeyer is invited to leave home to discover her or his own path, to meet her or his own limitations, and to find her or his own gifts. The process is different for each person, but the pattern is the same. The meaning of the process for the journeyer is to find the particular treasure, the individual mission, that is hers or his alone and to return home bringing back this special gift for the benefit of all.

On this journey, there is also the inevitable dragon that one must slay before reaching the treasure. When people coming to age have been tutored long enough by life, they may be able to recognize and confront the internal and external dragons that are holding them back from reaching their full potential. They may be able to relate to those things that would hold them back in such a way as to lessen their destructive power. And in confronting these things that hold them back, they may find embedded in the struggle the very things they lack. For example, if my dragon is fear, I must recognize the particular way that fear comes to me and confront it. In the confronting of it, not only will I lessen its effect on my ability to function, but I will find the treasures of courage and self-confidence as well.

The archetypal journey is a general pattern in the lives of all people, although it is individual to each person as well. It is influenced by many factors, including personal attributes, family and culture, and gender, as well as by typology. In the language of type development, the heroic journey concentrates in the early life on the adequate development of the preferences indicated by one's four-letter type code. The good development of the dominant and auxiliary functions can help people establish a strong ego—a solid sense of who they are and how they can function. And later, when this development has carried the journeyer as far as it can, then some development of tertiary and inferior functions is required. Speaking typologically, it is often the lack of good access to the gifts of our nonpreferred functions or the gifts of any undeveloped functions (preferred or not) that holds us back from being and doing all that we have the potential to be and do. Our undeveloped functions can feel like dragons—but these dragons can mark the gateway to the treasure. Developing the less preferred parts of ourselves can teach us about limitation and humility as well, since each of us is not only gifted but also limited by our typological structure. We are well advised not to attempt to become the person represented by our nonpreferred functions, but it is also important not to exclude or repress this side of ourselves. Life can indeed, as Florida Scott-Maxwell says, change us, improve us, and leave us the same. Our challenge is to recognize and participate in the process.

In part 2, we will explore some diverse life journeys. Using Jungian typology as our organizing principle, we will look at the journeys of some creative people coming to age. I have arranged the interviews according to the four mental function pairs described by Jung—that is, Intuition and Feeling, Sensing and Thinking, Intuition and Thinking, and Sensing and Feeling. People, of course, vary within as well as between these categories, and I have not forced consistency. You may find that the type categories can deepen your understanding, or you may simply wish to learn from the beautiful snapshots of creative people coming to age.

Come eavesdrop as people with different types talk about their life journeys. Listen as these people speak of their long lives, of their gifts, and of their limitations. Listen as they talk of coming to age, of what makes meaning for them in this stage of life, and of how they prepare for the future, including, when the time is right, the final letting go of life. Listen as they speak of their surprise and delight as they discover some of the unexpected joys of the later years—contentment, generosity, spaciousness, joy, devotion, connectedness, relatedness, and vitality—and as they acknowledge them with gratitude.

CHAPTER 4

VITALITY
AND CONTENTMENT

I think somehow, we learn who we really are

and then live with that decision.

—Eleanor Roosevelt

NF Vitality and contentment are two of the unexpected joys of the later years for these idealistic people whose lives are marked by desire for personal growth and harmonious relationships—characteristics associated with preferences for Intuition and Feeling. As these people age, they seem to have an increasing ability to know the limits of self-knowledge and intimate relationship while still treasuring both. Their capacity to hold the tension between passion and tranquility grows. They recognize the importance of living in the present and of limiting experience without losing the color of life. They find the ability to keep a balance between withdrawing from and demanding too much of life. For those who prefer Intuition and Feeling, creatively coming to age means learning to live what life allows, with all its joys and tears.

$\mathcal{T}$he well-developed Intuitive Feeling types (INFJ, ENFJ, INFP, ENFP) have been described as catalysts, seekers, idealists, and self-actualizers. They are people of imagination and passion for whom the search for self-understanding, personal growth, and meaning are lifelong interests. They are empathetic, caring people who greatly value harmony and can be fascinating and energizing. In my interviews, I found myself dealing with people who bring color and music to life—whether they are softspoken and hesitant, struggling for a few words to articulate their deepest thoughts, feelings, and images, or whether they bubble with words, stories, and enthusiasm. Their lives are usually marked by intensity and sometimes by discontent—or at least a search for more. They seek answers to ultimate questions, and they seek acceptance, affirmation, and understanding—sometimes more than can be given.

Their lives are usually marked by intensity and sometimes by discontent— or at least a search for more.

Children preferring Intuition and Feeling are generally idealistic, imaginative, pleasant, and loving. They like to please others, particularly the INFJs, ENFJs, and ENFPs, and may go to great lengths to do so. The INFPs like to please, too, but they often work to discover how, as one person suggested, "to please others as we pursue our private paths."

At midlife, these people, often more than many other types, recognize that their lives need to change. Much of the turmoil they feel revolves around the pressure the midlife transition brings to become more aligned with one's authentic being and the resulting tension this may bring to relationships with family, culture, and oneself. How to be oneself and live harmoniously with others, a question for most people, is particularly important for people who rely on their Intuition and Feeling preferences. Their natural desires to delve deeply into themselves, to avoid conflict, and to be accepted bring added poignancy. At midlife, these people also have to learn to confront the necessity to live in the ordinariness of life and to live in a less than perfect world. They would do well to attend to the note attached to one person's refrigerator that read, "If you want to be loved, then take human nature as it is." Yet it is essential that they retain their natural idealism, hope, and enthusiasm as well.

When these idealistic, loving, self-actualizing Intuitive Feeling people learn to accept the limits imposed by contact with real people and everyday culture, they find their later lives marked by contentment as well as passion. They are not as likely to be burdened and held back by cynicism that can lead to withdrawal or to overbearing behavior. They are also less likely to demand more extraordinary experiences, insights, and relationships than are possible and that can divert their attention from the ordinary and the specific that their own particular life may be calling them to.

As they age creatively, these people may come to see that although they cannot love the world into their vision of what it should be, they can live in the world as it is, and even love it as it is, while holding on to their hope and vision. They learn that they cannot be totally accepted or understood by another anymore than they can totally accept and understand anyone else; in the face of this, they can nevertheless love themselves and others. And as they are able to meet the coldness, the meanness, the lack of color that they see around them without turning away in withdrawal or cynicism or attacking with self-righteousness, they may find they can also hear and feel the music and mystery of life. Others may feel more adequate and less pressured in their presence.

Intuitive Feeling people who are aging creatively learn that life requires them to make realistic and limiting choices, even as they guard the passion that sings in their blood. As they contain the tendency that can drive them to desire more and more of everything they lack, they come to cherish what they have or can find close at hand. And they may be surprised and delighted to discover the gifts of vitality and contentment—gifts rarely available to the idealistic and loving Intuitive Feeling people when they are young.

Vital contentment is not complacency; rather, it is the ability to limit excessive desires and demands. It comes to the Intuitive Feeling people when they find they can love without requiring that the recipient of the love be deserving or that the love be returned. Contentment comes when they realize the folly of giving themselves away to please others or expecting others to relinquish themselves to meet their needs. Contentment is the ability to continue one's journey, but without excessive striving and struggle. It is being able to stay on one's journey toward love without insecurity or self-righteousness.

Vitality and contentment come to Intuitive Feeling people when they realize that every moment is precious. It comes when they are able to live in the moment without being attached to the moment. They know the joys of the present and of the senses when they can recognize the beauty in the color of that first azalea blossom or the spiritual peace of watching a sunset. They experience vitality and contentment when a fleeting moment of true intimacy with another human being brings them close to paradise or when they can accept things as they are without giving up hope.

This contentment is not sloth. It is alive and passionate, but it is also accepting. One INFP summed this up eloquently when she said, "I want peace and I want passion. The contentment is that I'm learning to accept that I want both."

Vitality and contentment come with the acceptance of personal limitations. This acceptance can have to do with a body that doesn't work as it once did. It can also have to do with recognizing the low points of life and the dark side of one's personhood as opportunities for growth. Ultimately, vital contentment comes with knowing that one has lived the life one was given to live and that nothing more is required.

Now I'd like you to meet a few of these creatively aging Intuitive Feeling people. Listen closely, and you will hear how life has changed them and how it has left them the same.

BETH AND MARIE—INFPs

Beth, Age 62

Beth is a woman of many talents who is vitally involved in her community. She has worked for almost a decade with aging people and is known locally as an expert on aging. She is alive, vibrant, extremely active, and known for her organizational abilities as well as for her teaching, musical, and writing talents. The energy she brings to situations combined with her youthful appearance make her age of sixty-two a surprise to many people. Her psychological type description is INFP.

> *College and my early work life in a big metropolitan city were a thriving time. At age twenty-nine, with the biological urge to reproduce driving me, I married, had children, and went to sleep. I loved my husband, my children, my job, and the master's degree I earned, but I wasn't happy. Yet I had all these good things, so I tried to keep on going. By the time I earned my advanced degree, I had to face*

my unhappiness. I was in my early forties, and I was overweight and unhappy. Following a hysterectomy and a scary but necessary divorce, I fell apart emotionally. Then I discovered alcohol. I could go for long periods without drinking, but at crisis times—or, strangely, at really happy times—I would cope by falling back on alcohol. I thought if I could do good things and live an independent life, I wouldn't have to face the alcohol issue. At age fifty-five, I was persuaded to check into a hospital for alcohol treatment. While in my hospital bed, I picked up my journal and began to write. It was the beginning of the way back to myself.

She explained that during those years of going through the motions necessary for a successful life, the real Beth was asleep under a hard outer shell. This outer shell, her achiever, was good at and often enjoyed what it did. But it had little contact with the drunk nonachiever who lived inside. Then one day she had this dream:

Someone took my car by mistake and I took another's car by mistake. I liked the car I took and didn't realize it wasn't mine for quite a while. I got it innocently, but it wasn't my car. I got held back by driving other people's cars.

This was a profound moment of realization for Beth—she needed to be driving her own car. She is still involved in a

> **"I do a lot, but I'm less uptight, less perfectionistic."**

great many things these days, but with a different attitude: "I do a lot, but I'm less uptight, more in control, less perfectionistic. I'm going to do the best I can, but not sweat and overprepare. My best is all you can ask of me." Beth feels she is no longer asleep.

Marie, Age 70

This sense of getting caught in others' agendas is also understandable to Marie, another INFP. Marie is a vital woman of seventy years who models the creative aging process for many to observe. Her hair is gray and she is a little round, although she is still quite athletic looking. She moves and speaks slowly and deliberately. She is committed to her work and to her friends, family, colleagues, and those she mentors.

Marie struggles with her inability to find the balance between doing the things that really matter to her and doing those things she considers necessary but not personally fulfilling. She struggles with her need for rest and relaxation and her desire to be a part of things that could contribute to a more "moral society." She accepts these struggles as "part of the process." Recognizing and accepting may be what leads to the sense of vital contentment people often feel in her presence.

For sixty years, my body did what I wanted it to do. By the age of sixty, it had gotten me to a safe place—and then it quit. In fact, it simply put me to bed. I couldn't count on it, and at first I felt betrayed. Then I realized I should thank it for serving me well for sixty years. When one door closes, another really can open. When I couldn't count on my body, I learned some things. My eyes were problematic, and I had to face the possibility of blindness. I am doing inner work—what I can—so I'll be prepared if I can't see, and I'm doing practical things, too, such as learning to listen to tapes. I've always been very visual, so I have to train myself to be auditory. I've had some other problems with my body, and I decided not to chase physicians around. I know what to do. I need to under-schedule. I'm fine if I pace myself, and if I don't, I pay. And inter-estingly, with better pacing, life is more vivid.

Marie speaks freely of death.

Most people are dead before they are 100, and I don't want to pre-tend death isn't going to happen. To pretend that cheats us. My greediness for life may come from this realization. You don't know about tomorrow at 70, and I want to live in the present. There is a vividness about this. A friend asked me recently if I didn't think things were getting more vivid. I do think so, and knowledge of death as a personal reality is a part of this. I remember reading Erik Erikson, who said we can't live until we can give up the fear of death.

She went on to speak of the idea of later life as preparation for death, which once might have seemed a morbid concept to her, but no longer. "I'm slowly understanding the wheel of life. I'm finally getting in touch with the rhythm. It's a slowly dawning understanding."

And there is an understanding and acceptance of paradox. She understands the difference between appropriate struggle and being caught in struggle. "I've spent my whole life going after God," Marie laughed. "Maybe all we have to do is be open, sit quietly, and accept the Mystery." She

"You don't know about tomorrow at 70, and I want to live in the present."

explained that acceptance is not caving in but being humble with dignity. In fact she sees humility and dignity as two sides of the same coin, and that led to a discussion of the importance of paradox.

> *Someone once told me you cannot understand life until you can delight in paradox and delight in a mischievous Creator. Truth is like a crystal with many facets, and we come to it through our own facet. This is why personality type matters so much to me. It's a valid way of seeing differences. We can learn our own way and see others' ways, and then we can grow our own way and bond with others who grow their own ways. When our children were growing up, we often had foreign exchange students in our home. They could bring a different view and shake us up a bit. We could grow. We didn't become them or accept everything they represented, but we could learn parts from them. Understanding personality type is like that.*

This sounded like a life passion. And it did not seem to be diminishing with age. Marie's passion is for a world where people treat one another with true respect.

> *True respect is about love. It requires some letting go of one's own needs in order to love the other persons as they are. The realization of the difficulty of this task of loving others as they are has led me to some understanding of the "miserable sinner" language from my early religious training. I used to hate those words,* miserable sinners, *but we are. It is good to be able to say I blew it again and I'm forgiven again. Now I do have to acknowledge how I hurt people and I have to have the intention of doing better, but I can't do it. It's too hard, and I'm forgiven over and over when I fail.*

So this impossible-to-achieve sense of true respect for others is a passion. What does this woman fear? It is not so much personal fear that my question elicits. She fears "for our culture." She sees our culture as "materialistic, meanspirited, greedy, and hypocritical." She fears for psychology (her field) when she watches it basing its practice on diagnosis and assuming that there is some norm to which all people should aspire. She fears for religion, which has omitted the mystical tradition, and for the misplaced emphasis of Christianity, which highlights the sacrificial savior Jesus as opposed to the Jesus as guide who can show the way of life to any who can hear.

Coming to Age as an INFP

These creative, optimistic INFPs, as they age, do not waste time ruminating over lost opportunities or vacillating. They are able to make choices and act. "I never let myself off the hook because I can't do something or get stopped by my fears that someone will fail to appreciate what I'm doing or even that I have to do it right," says Marie. "I act." And Beth agrees:

> I really love being alive in spite of it all. I'm aware of death and I treasure life. I don't have time to fool around. If it's a good idea, do it. I don't ask, Why me? Life is as it is, and you make the best of it.

They have learned to be and act in the face of things that could hold them back, as Marie points out:

> I've spent my life hurting for people, but I realize now that I need to have a piece of me that accepts the reality of what's out there. I can cry over the tragedies in the newspaper every morning, but then I need to get on with my day.

Getting on with life has a great deal to do with an awareness of the limitations of resources, particularly time and energy. Marie speaks of the later years as being more "vivid." When one becomes aware that one's days are limited, even the most ordinary things and the most ordinary people of each day can take on added significance. There is a sweet contentment that comes from setting limits and committing only to what really matters.

Seeing things as they are while wishing for something better, and seeing the darkness in themselves and others while loving themselves and others anyway, are simply "the way things are" for INFPs. They are part of the paradox. And the acceptance of the need to live in this tension brings a sense of contentment. "This balance problem will probably be a problem until I die—and in a way, I hope it is," smiled Marie. "It's a paradox, this inner and outer. I want peace and balance, but I also want passion. I just must accept this." And in this learning may lie the sense of vital contentment rarely available to these INFPs when they are young.

MARGARET, SHELBY, AND LOIS—ENFPs

Margaret, Age 74

The walls of Margaret's home are covered with her paintings, books, and treasures from seventy-four years of full

> *"I wish someone had told me to be myself."*

living. She shares the home with her husband of many years and is often visited by grown children, grandchildren, and her many friends. She occasionally teaches an art workshop or a creative journaling workshop. Her psychological type is ENFP.

"I wish someone had told me to be myself," Margaret began. "I thought doing God's will was doing what other people wanted. But this is what hell is—being obligated to be other than oneself."

Margaret's life for some years has been a slow letting go of things that obligated her to be other than herself. At thirty-eight, as an executive's wife, she followed her husband to a new location. This move gave her the opportunity to begin "to drop things off." She had felt particularly "gobbled up" by her church, the same church that had acted as a warm, supportive family when she experienced the loss of a baby and her mother in her early thirties. But now it was time to let some things go, to learn that limits had to be set.

> We all have to clip our wings. In any case, I started saying "I can't" and then learned to say "I won't." With the "I won't" came a sense of integrity. I want to tell young folks to be themselves and not to spread themselves too thin, but I also want to tell them to find their passion. I have creative energy, and if you have creative energy and you don't use it, it will kill you. It will make you physically ill.

This "dropping things off" happened slowly for her, but by forty-eight she felt she didn't have to meet everyone's expectations, and by sixty she felt she had "paid her dues" and was free to live her own life.

By sixty-five this attitude was really in place, and by seventy it was absolutely solid. "Now," she told me, "others matter, but I always ask myself if I really want to do something before I agree."

It was easy to see that Margaret appreciates and enjoys life, despite some hardships. Her life is marked by passion and by acceptance and commitment. She has learned that small is beautiful and that limits can be lived with creatively.

Things happen and we have to make the best of them. At fifty-five, I had to enter the hospital. I was teaching nine yoga classes at that time, and they were important to me for they gave me, besides some income, a sense of status and identity. I have only a high school diploma, and these classes helped me feel competent. After I was hospitalized, I knew I couldn't teach anymore. I had to suffer that, and I had to learn I'm limited. There are things I can't do, but there are many things I can do. Sometimes when I've done a bad picture, I cut it up. Parts of it often make wonderful miniatures. We can make beautiful miniatures with the good parts of life.

Shelby, Age 64

Shelby, slightly younger than Margaret and also an ENFP, knows, too, that small is beautiful. She is interested in "helping people learn to live simply" precisely so that they can be free to live their real passions. Widely known as a proponent of creative aging, Shelby is a woman who lives her passion. She has long been interested in creative aging because of her training in sociology and her work in an agency for aging, but now, at sixty-four, she has a personal interest as well.

"We must learn to choose consciously."

She is officially retired, although it does not seem so when one observes her life. She has formed a small company to provide some necessary income, she leads seminars on such topics as using leisure time well and voluntary simplicity, and she heads up outdoor activities such as hikes and bike trips. Her enthusiasm and authenticity are attributes one notices immediately. Shelby values personal freedom and is taking the small, concrete steps required to make this happen. This means making choices in order to do what really matters to her.

"In my seminars," she says, "I talk about retirees who go from the work ethic to the busy ethic. If life is busy, then life is justified, it seems. There is danger in this. We must learn to choose consciously." Shelby has chosen consciously to do the work that makes her happy and that is, at the same time, attacking society's obsession with materialism and its lack of respect for the human spirit. Her retirement plan received "very little support" from friends who recognized Shelby's precarious financial position and feared the reduction of retirement funds. Shelby had another way of reasoning, perhaps an ENFP way, laden with values and a passionate love of adventure:

> I just weighed my personal freedom and happiness against the financial security. I thought to myself, "You'd better do what you want at sixty, for you might not be able to do it at seventy, and if you are still able to do it at seventy, then you can do it again." I wanted to ride my bike across the country, and I wanted to walk the Appalachian Trail. I did the former but couldn't complete the latter because of a leg fracture. I was really down about this, but I made another bike trip, and I walk some of the trail each year. I pick myself up.

The natural world is Shelby's passion. It "cuts through the crap and it feels good to be able to observe the birds, the flowers, the textures. It feels good to be in good physical shape."

Lois, Age 63

Lois had raised a large family and was recently retired from a thriving counseling practice. She was a small woman, fit, active, and alert, and I immediately

> "My humor and outrageousness help me get by."

felt the energy she generated. "My family loves me, but they think I'm nuts," she confessed. "My humor and outrageousness help me get by." Lois is an energetic, life-affirming ENFP with passionate ups and downs that she doesn't deny.

> I have regrets about a lot of things and I don't deny them, but I don't live there either. Challenges are the growing edge of life, and for me, being on the growing edge is more important than being happy, successful, or well-adjusted. Challenges got me two master's degrees. Without challenges I might be playing tennis all day. Growing is what it's about. I feel alienated from my family because of this, and I've spent my life trying to please and take care of them and others. But I do this less now. I look now at every life decision with the

thought that I might not have but another twenty years, if that.
So I set priorities, and one is whom I spend my time with. I say, if I
don't want to spend time with someone, let someone else love that one.

And aliveness is important, too, says Lois. She is doing some writing, and she told me about a recent haiku she had written to her amaryllis.

I bought a beautiful and too expensive leather journal recently.
I call it my special journal. And in it I wrote to my amaryllis. I love
that plant. It colors outside the lines. Here in the bleakness of win-
ter, it blooms. Everything is supposed to be dead, and here is this
outrageous amaryllis that hasn't got any better sense than to bloom
like crazy. I love that amaryllis.

Coming to Age as an ENFP

How do these adventurous, freedom-loving people bring meaning to their experiences? Do they see themselves as connected to anything spiritual beyond themselves? How do they feel about the ending of life, about death and dying? Margaret, who says she has been living tentatively for twenty years, speaks openly without prompting about such things.

I'm not happy all the time. I have fears. I fear bodily decline and
hope I'll always be cared for. I fear I'll lose my husband or family or
suffer a prolonged death. With my health problems, my heart is in
control and my life is planned around it. But I don't fear death.
Having a near-death experience has relieved that. People say these
near-death experiences are physiological, but I don't mind what
they say. I've seen the other side. I hope I die suddenly.

The vivacious, active Shelby feels this way about facing death:

When I think of dying, which I don't very often, I'm sad. I'm going
to die. My time on Earth is limited. But I don't want to die. I want
to live forever, for I have things to do. This knowledge, however, does
make me a little more in touch with myself and what I can do. I
want to use my time thoroughly, and I want to do what I really can
do. I'm a little more meditative now. . . . If I want to believe in a

Greater Power, nature is what convinces me. Wonderful things happen in nature, and I find solace there. I'm a little more content now.

And the humorous and outrageous Lois has come to these conclusions:

I'm not afraid of dying, but I am afraid of not living to the fullest potential I can. You can't always live to your potential, for there are times when you simply don't have the reins and you just have to ride things out on the rump. Nevertheless, later life fulfillment is about being conscious. It's not about worrying about every ache and pain, but about passion. I wake every morning saying, "Thank you, God, for letting me be alive. What's in store for today?"

Age has brought Margaret, Lois, Shelby, and many other ENFPs a slower pace, and with it, more self-awareness. They often find, in looking back, that they can discern a pattern to their lives—a pattern that could not be seen as they were rushing to embrace the world and to experience everything. They also came to see the dangers in extremes and the need to weigh consequences. They learned the need for commitment. Margaret spoke of her belief that things do work together for good, but berated those with a view of life in which "they think they have it all in a box."

Well, life blasts that. Things do work together for good, but not in a Pollyanna way. It has more to do with people who live truthfully with love. It means things are happening, things are stirring. It means things aren't fixed, but moving. As the Zen Buddhists know, everything is as it should be and everything is changing. It is hard to know this when you are young.

MIRIAM AND MICHAEL—INFJs

Miriam, Age 72

Miriam, whose psychological type is INFJ, is from a large immigrant family. Her father came to this country when the Depression hit Europe in the 1920s, and his wife and their many children followed later. Six weeks after her mother arrived in this country, Miriam's father died, leaving the family impoverished. Although she was an excellent student, Miriam left school at sixteen to pay her own way. Later she married a professional man, and in her late thirties, while caring for small children, she earned her GED and her college degree with honors. She felt these school years, despite the hard work and her fear that she couldn't do the work, to be some of the best of her life.

I got confidence from returning to school, and I enjoyed the learning —and maybe I just did it to improve myself. I've always wanted to improve myself, but that is something I've come to terms with as I've aged. I've always felt inadequate and surrounded myself with people who, in my mind, were more worthwhile. That's changed, too. I've come to realize that I just thought they had it all and didn't have to struggle. We all have to struggle.

So what is struggle like for this woman now that she knows everyone has to struggle? Is she happy?

I know myself well enough to know that if I weren't sometimes unhappy in one place I would be unhappy in another. Life is about getting through, enduring what comes and finding moments of pleasure. I can't stand people who are happy all the time. They're deniers. They wear me out, though maybe they can't help it. That's how they function. We all function some way.

Recognizing her proclivity toward insecurity and making some peace with this tendency has led directly to contentment. "Aging people age as they have lived—that is, they become more what they always were. . . . The older we get, the more the veneer wears off and we become what was always under it." This insight seems to bring her peace. She no longer feels the inferiority struggle and the kind of overarching passion she once did. It is not, of course, that there is no passion, but it is "passion removed from the fray." She finds happiness in that which is smaller and close at hand. She continues.

> **"The older we get, the more the veneer wears off and we become what was always under it."**

My sense of joy is different. I love my solo time. I'm on an even keel. If the garden looks good, it's a nice day. Sometimes something I read, or a piece of music I hear, really moves me. Real contact with my few really good friends gives me pleasure. These friends can really talk about things that matter—not superficial things. I can trust my true feelings, which sometimes aren't nice, with them. I don't have to hold back, and I won't be judged.

Michael, Age 68

Michael is a sixty-eight-year-old retired educator who has been married but currently lives alone. He is devoted to a community project designed to bring better science education to disadvantaged children. His psychological type is INFJ. Michael talks about passions connected to things ordinary and things close at hand. He talks about the need to keep life simple and unencumbered in order to be free to do the things that really matter to him. He is financially satisfied. "I live so that I have more money than I need." And although many would see him as a man of passion, he talks about serenity. He speaks softly and thoughtfully. "I'm in a serene place," he begins. "I don't have to prove anything to anyone, and it's okay to die." It had not always been that way for Michael.

One day, some years ago now, I had a crashing insight. All at once, I was absolutely clear that I and all that I knew would one day be obliterated. That kept me awake at night for ten years.

He talked about his experience with issues of death and dying and his journey to serenity.

I had to face death directly when my wife suffered a crushing stroke. It was about five o'clock one afternoon, and I was on my way out of town for a job interview. My wife, the mother of our two small children, complained of an excruciating headache. By six o'clock, an emergency room doctor was telling me my wife had had a stroke and I was to prepare to say good-bye to her. In one hour my world turned upside down, although she lived for another seventeen years, largely in an unconscious state.

Those years were a time of caring, not only for her but for the children. Times were difficult, of course, but the years also brought much joy. "I really have no regrets about what I did or didn't do. Life is what it is," he told me.

> "I really have no regrets. . . . Life is what it is."

Coming to Age as an INFJ

How do individualistic, thoughtful, complex INFJs in their sixties and seventies make meaning out of their lives and prepare for the end of them? Michael's faith has helped him make sense out of life.

> *God is within, and we come to God through ourselves, and we con-nect with each other through that of God in each of us. I like the image of a tree to explain this. We're the leaves and we're connected through the trunk, an existence that is outside ourselves but to which we are connected, to the other leaves. That's how it feels to me. . . . My life is a prayer—I don't need to join with people to seek, and I don't spend time in prayer. Living is prayer. There's not truth apart from the search for it.*

Miriam, too, finds some sense of integrity in her own individualis-tic way. "We're all part of everything and we can't depend on things out-side ourselves. I have great reverence for the mystery of the universe."

These visionary and passionate INFJs have come to know content-ment while retaining the song of life, as Michael so well exemplifies.

> *There is always the search, but you can be serene when you're in tune and on track. You know life will give laughter and tears and that both are okay. When I feel bad, it opens me. What happens is, and "what is" is okay. I live with it all. . . . Health problems can be bothersome, of course, but I don't really fear incapacitation. My wife taught me about that. When we're stripped of our functionali-ty, we can express spirit. One can be physically debilitated and get more beautiful, more loved, and more loving. I couldn't have pre-dicted what I could have done in my life and can't predict what I'll do, but maybe I'll handle whatever it is that comes up. I sleep well.*

BERNIE, CARL, AND BARBARA—ENFJs

Bernie, Age 79

Bernie, at age seventy-nine, is known for his many contributions to his church, his community, and the retirement center that he recently entered with his wife. His career field prior to his retirement was advertising, and people speak of him as a caring, public-minded man with many friends and broad interests. His psychological type is ENFJ.

"I'm interested in public affairs," Bernie began. Though he is new to the retirement center, he has already organized a current topics group, and he brings in speakers from a variety of backgrounds. He likes his living arrangement because people are involved in the planning, and "if you want something done you do it." He likes to contribute and has difficulty with others "who don't feel any need to contribute or even to speak up and let people know what they think." He is also bothered by people who do not respond to others' needs, or at least, "let them know you care." These characteristics probably have not changed much over the years for Bernie, but some others have.

> *"At least let them know you care."*

> *I'm more tolerant and I do accept more than I used to. Sometimes I can even accept that there are limits to what a person can do or even to how a person can think. Yet I'm still sometimes annoyed if people don't say what they think or act on what they believe. I'm also more cautious about offering advice. And although I like to have something to do each day, I don't have to. That's a change.*

Bernie told me an amusing story that illustrates a mature understanding of overinvolvement rarely available to the younger ENFJ.

> *I was out walking one day when I saw some people working on a sewer. They looked like they had a problem, so I made a suggestion. That's my inclination. The workmen said "good idea." I knew at that moment I'd better get out of there because they were going to take my advice. I knew nothing whatsoever about sewers. Nevertheless, I was taking some responsibility for doing something.*

Carl, Age 62

Carl is a sixty-two-year-old man, described by his multitude of friends and followers as outgoing, interesting, and charming. His psychological type is ENFJ. I asked Carl how he is different from the way he was several decades ago and how he handles things differently. He talked about being less controlling, more cautious, and more appreciative of the sensory side of life.

> *"I now have, on a scale of zero to ten, somewhere between a zero and one need to change people."*

I live life to the fullest. I'm less compulsive and less controlling than I once was, and I appreciate life. I now have, on a scale of zero to ten, somewhere between a zero and one need to change people. That's a change. I used to have to save the wounded. When I was doing a lot of counseling, which I don't do now, if you had a problem and didn't come to me, I was hurt; and if you came to me and didn't get better, I felt I screwed up. Now I still try to be helpful and I don't want to stop that, but it is up to you whether you take the help or not. It's so refreshing. I say no. I set limits on rescuing, and it's all in the frame of reference of responsibility.

I'm still interested in growing. After all, if you don't grow you die, but I've become a little more choosy about my growing. There was a time when I would try anything that was even remotely connected to growth—acupuncture, marijuana, goldfish eating, whatever it was, if it was remotely related to growth, I would try it. And I learned a lot, but I'm more choosy about my growth experiences now. I do smell a few more daisies now, too. For example, last spring I gave my wife a shock. As I was backing out of my driveway one morning, I realized the gorgeous azaleas were in their very last stages. I stopped and said good-bye to them. I said "Good-bye, azaleas, I'll see you next spring." I couldn't have allowed that twenty years ago. It probably took Rolfing and acupuncture and goldfish eating to get me into life—to get me to the place where I could experience the sensory side of life.

Barbara, Age 64

Barbara is an ENFP mother who, several years ago, suffered the tragic loss of her teenage daughter in an automobile accident. The loss taught her about the limits of involvement and about real unconditional love. Her daughter had been returning to college with her boyfriend after a weekend visit to his parents, and he had fallen asleep at the wheel of his car. He was not injured, but Barbara's daughter died. Barbara defines unconditional love as love without demand that others conform to one's own desires. She spoke of this time after the accident when, although she had great need, she found that she could not demand of another what that person could not give.

> *Unconditional love is love without demand that others conform to one's own desires.*

This time after the accident was a hard time for me, and for my husband and my marriage as well. My husband just couldn't talk or respond in a way that supported me. But I had a wonderful, strong mother, and if it hadn't been for her I might not have been able to make it through that death.

Some years after the tragic accident, Barbara finally let go of her bitterness and contacted her daughter's boyfriend.

He had married and had been in therapy. When he called I simply said what I wanted to say: "You are forgiven." He said he would like to come to see us and bring his wife, and I told him we would be glad to see him, but he didn't need to come—that he was totally forgiven. And I was able to tell him that I hoped he'd treat his wife as he would have treated my daughter. He loved my daughter and treated her well. The car wreck was an accident, but I'll tell you that the forgiveness didn't come from me. It came from Someone else. I think how hard it must be for him to accept this forgiveness. . . . And I'm so grateful I can forgive him. What an awful legacy a bitter mother and a boyfriend unable to live his life would be to my beautiful, loving daughter.

Coming to Age as an ENFJ

The ability to stand at some distance from relationships and the decreasing tendency to make demands on others can bring relief to the ENFJs. They become more willing to be part of the world and not in charge of it. With this lessening of the need to be in charge or to "save the wounded," the ENFJs are often surprised and delighted to find an increasing ability to relax, to contemplate, and to develop more personal insight. They are often surprised—and delighted—to discover they have fallen upon a sense of deep peace and contentment. These seekers of self-awareness and relationship often speak of having made some peace in matters of relationships, as does Carl: "I'm a failure in some ways, and I can't fix that. But I've learned to live with it. I'm no longer guilty and I don't kick myself around. I've made some peace. I've talked to my kids and owned some of my faults. We've rebuilt some of our relationship, and there is some integrity and closeness."

And how do these dynamic, loving people in their sixties and seventies make sense of their lives as they come to age and closer to life's end? Carl takes life as it is.

> *I don't want to die, but I don't think I'm afraid of death. I couldn't be more confident in my relationship to my universe, and when my time comes to go, I'll be at peace. I'll probably go with a lot left undone and also with confidence that if I could I would order life again as it has been—or at least much as it has been. Faith has a lot to do with death, and we don't have to be religious. We can be anti-God for that matter, but we have to formulate some faith system. In the face of death, we can't deny, blame, or crumble. We don't need to worry about death if we take care of life. My relational life is preparing me for death. It has hellish and heavenly moments, and I can't escape these by getting out of relationships—or by dying, for that matter. Age gives me this perspective. You never know the day or the hour of death. I wouldn't have liked to leave life ten years ago with my relational life with my children being as it was.*

Barbara spoke of her philosophy and her hope for the end of life. "He'll give you the ticket when you're ready to get on the train," she responded. "People are supposed to die, but not to suffer." She talked about taking care of herself, but how she would like to find a doctor with "the right pill" when it is time to go.

Although Barbara was obviously concerned about the process of dying, she felt death itself should be a celebration. Barbara told me of the funeral of her grandchildren's other grandmother.

> *We had a funeral, sat on chairs by the grave, and read Bible verses. But afterward I bought a big helium balloon, and we had a celebration. We let the balloon go and float up toward the sky as a housewarming gift for grandmother in her new home.*

CONCLUSION

Speaking generally, how would we say the creative people presented in the interviews in this chapter have changed? How are they different in the coming to age period of life than in earlier life? What are the unexpected joys of the later years? I suggest they are vitality and contentment. Creative Intuitive Feeling people coming to age hold the tension between serenity and passion. They limit excessive demands for love. They no longer expect to be loved—or to love—perfectly. They more fully accept themselves and require less of others. They live in the present and delight in the joys of the senses. They accept what life allows.

CHAPTER 5

GENEROSITY
AND SPACIOUSNESS

I had thought . . . that whatever was worth
accomplishing in life could be accomplished
by reason and will.

—Oliver Sacks

ST Generosity and spaciousness are often unexpected joys of the later years for these practical people who focus on clarity, action, what they can know through their senses, and what they can accomplish through their willpower—characteristics associated with preferences for Sensing and Thinking. As they age, these people tend to view life through an expanded lens, and their increasingly open hearts allow them to entertain ambiguity, complexity, and divergent points of view—even as they claim their own. For people who prefer Sensing and Thinking, creatively coming to age means learning to give back, for they realize that so much has been given to them.

The well-developed Sensing Thinking types (ISTJ, ESTJ, ISTP, ESTP) are often described as practical, logical, and present oriented. They are the producers of the world. Whether in the more planful, deliberate manner of ISTJ and ESTJ or the more immediate, playful manner of ISTP and ESTP, they know how to get the job done. Interviews with them are usually marked by preparation on their part, an economy of words, and often a great deal of humor. They are usually gifted with an ability to see just what needs to be done in the moment, and when they understand what is needed, they are ready to respond. In fact, for people who prefer using Sensing with Thinking, it is in the responding, rather than in the anticipating, that tension is relieved and fulfillment is found. When asked what they want to be remembered for, a common response is, "I did what I could." They focus on the present and on what they know. As one person said, they "dream the possible dream"—and they may sometimes dream a dream too small.

> They have even learned to entertain some ultimate questions, though sometimes classifying them as "silly things to worry about."

As children, they are often seen by parents and teachers as determined, curious, and focused. They want to know how things work in precise detail, for they believe what they can experience and what they can understand and explain. Sometimes they accept only those things that make sense to them. This may annoy parents and teachers, although Sensing Thinking children may also be acknowledged for this curious nature and for their ability to get the job done.

At midlife, Sensing Thinking people often notice that their bodies are not behaving as they used to, but they rarely acknowledge a midlife crisis. Things can occasionally feel too restricted or too out of hand, but more often it takes something dramatic or someone important to them to get their attention. Rarely do they consciously ask "ultimate questions"—or at least they do not ask ultimate questions until their experience puts the questions directly in their paths. Things such as work difficulties, relationship problems, and health breakdowns often interrupt the Sensing Thinking lifestyle, and they may find previously unnecessary questions taking on some urgency at these times.

Looking deeper and more extensively into themselves and nurturing their relationships with others may help the hardworking, active Sensing Thinking people avoid falling into the trap of discounting, which can prevent them from learning what life has to offer. Discounting, that is, not attending to or sufficiently valuing things, can take different forms. The creatively aging Sensing Thinking people have learned not to discount everything that is outside their particular focus or goal or that interferes with the pace they have set for themselves. They have learned not to discount others' opinions and wishes. They have even learned to entertain some ultimate questions, though sometimes classifying them as "silly things to worry about." In doing this, many Sensing Thinking people coming to age are less likely to miss the scenery, the deeper complexity, and the ambiguity that can enrich life. They are able to recognize the complexity and the mystery of intimacy and relationship with others and with themselves that can bring them depth, breadth, and joy.

As these autonomous, practical, inventive people age, expanding the lens through which they view the world and opening their hearts helps them become more spacious and gracious people. They find themselves more spacious in that they are increasingly able to embrace different views and styles without judging or needing to adopt them as their own. They find themselves more able to accept others' views as legitimate, even when these views don't meet the standards of logical analysis required by Sensing Thinking people. This more accepting and generous attitude is often expressed by saying something like "I don't understand it, but I guess it is good for them." One Sensing Thinking woman I interviewed came to this conclusion over the years regarding a family member with whom she had had a long-standing disagreement: "I've spent my life fighting what he is advocating, but I must say that I think he believes he is right. Perhaps I would also had I been raised in his part of the country at the time he was young."

Creatively aging Sensing Thinking people can become spacious enough to accept and embrace parts of themselves that were previously unavailable to them, particularly their imaginations and their emotions. Often to their surprise and delight, they find that they possess the ability to hope for, trust, imagine, and care about those things they cannot explain, while maintaining a healthy dose of skepticism. It may be that the wisdom of the years brings this expansion, but it also seems that living in different cultural environments, foreign travel, or anything else that encourages living with differences proves particularly growth producing for the Sensing Thinking people.

They often stretch their minds wide enough to embrace ambiguity and not feel overwhelmed by it. As one bank executive said, "I've come to recognize the existence of gray areas. I didn't used to accept gray, and even now there are poles. The poles are not gray; they are truth and integrity. Truth and integrity are the things that pull one back from drowning in too much gray." As they stretch their vision and open their hearts while holding onto truth and integrity, they may be suprised and delighted to discover the joys of spaciousness and generosity—joys rarely available to the focused, pragmatic STs when they are young.

Generosity and spaciousness are about sharing, openness, and abundance. With an increasing generosity of spirit, the Sensing Thinking people can open and expand. They can find that they have more room and are less constricted. They can make room for the ambiguity and complexity that enrich life. Their interests can broaden, and they can become more engaged by life. They become more interesting to others.

With increasing generosity of spirit, the Sensing Thinking judgment can soften. Right and wrong sometimes become harder to distinguish, and they become less demanding of themselves and others. They hold themselves more gently, and they need fewer defenses. Others find them more gracious and feel more cherished in their presence.

These practical, realistic, nondemonstrative people rarely articulate these gifts of spaciousness and graciousness. When such things are pointed out to them, a typical comment is "So it is, but I didn't think much about it."

Generosity of spirit is often reflected in the work of creatively aging Sensing Thinking people. They recognize how much they have themselves been given, and they feel more grateful, more joyful, and more able to freely give. Many times I heard someone say in the interviews, "I've been so blessed; it pleases me to do this for others. It helps me to give back."

Now I'd like you to meet some of these creatively aging Sensing Thinking people, and learn about the gifts of generosity and spaciousness they found in their later years.

CLARK AND JOSEPH—ISTPs

Clark, Age 61

Clark is a tall, lanky, athletic-looking sixty-one-year-old business owner. He and his wife of thirty-five years have three grown children. Like many STPs, Clark is very aware of physical changes that affect his body as he comes to age. He is an active, independent man, and he does not want to be "rolled up." He is considered fun to be with by the many people who know him.

Clark isn't sure that he has anything interesting to say about creative aging. "I'm resisting sixty-one," he began, "although now we don't really have to get old for a long time. People at seventy used to be put out to pasture, but it is really a shame if you can't be active at seventy." He talked of the fact that he does not want to be in a retirement center, even a luxurious one, because he can't imagine the space confinement. Confinement would limit the activities he enjoys most at the beginning of his seventh decade: running, sailing, horseback riding, and golf. He talks about his need for freedom and his hopes for aging.

> *"People at seventy used to be put out to pasture, but it is really a shame if you can't be active at seventy."*

> My wife and I live next door to an old couple, and they do wander around some, perhaps not knowing quite what they're up to, but they don't bother anyone. You can put people like that in nursing homes and they'll soon be dead. I want to keep in shape. What I fear is losing my health and being restricted or treated like a basket case. I want to slow down my work, but not walk out the door. I'll take some time off, but I don't need all day off. I don't have specific things I want to do that I don't do now, but I want to change the segments of my life some—reduce the work block and make the other segments bigger. A lot of the young people now want to make it big in business and get out by forty-five or fifty. It's like they want to hit a homer with the bases loaded. That may work for them, but not for me. I'll keep working, but I want to have more time for being in the country and for being with my family. I want to become as complete a person as possible, but part of this may be beyond my control.

Clark speaks of a woman he admires. She's in her upper eighties, and she lives alone in her big house and goes to the coast for the summers. "When you go over to her house for a glass of wine with her, she is interesting and can talk about anything." He admires that, as opposed to those old folks "who block life out and have nothing left to discuss but the weather and what they had for lunch."

Joseph, Age 65

Joseph is a successful, independent, retired military officer. He lives a happy, active, and productive life with his wife in a small, rural mountain town he describes as a place "close to heaven." Joseph, an ISTP, is knowledgeable about the MBTI. He agrees to the interview—even though some of my questions sound "a little flaky"—but quickly tells me the interview cannot be on Monday, Tuesday, or Wednesday because those are the days he helps his friend sell apples. It is obvious

"I hate whining and I hate things like senior citizen's discounts for people who can afford to pay for themselves"

that Joseph likes to help people when they need it, but he says he does not like whining or people who whine. This apple selling is work that he does without pay, but from which he gets something. If he didn't have fun doing the apple selling, he assures me, he would not be doing it. And although he kids me a bit about my project, it is also obvious to me that Joseph wants to help me understand.

> *Life is different now, but you ask how it is different from how it used to be. I don't know about that because I don't know how I used to look at it. I guess I did notice around fifty-five that I had to wear glasses to see and sometimes I hurt where I hadn't hurt before. But I hate whining and I hate things like senior citizen's discounts. Senior citizens ought to be glad they're still alive and not have younger people paying for them if they can afford to pay for themselves. It bugs me when a senior citizen who can afford to pay buys a cheap ticket. I don't want to be a whiner looking for entitlements. Just yesterday, an eighty-eight-year-old man bought a bushel of apples and I offered to carry them to his car for him. He said he could still carry them himself and I was glad for him. I would be happy to grab those apples without hesitation to help an infirm person, but there's a difference between whining and real need.*

This attitude of self-motivation and sufficiency is not limited to apple selling. Joseph's career was long and successful, and when he relates it in detail, assignment by assignment, it is obvious that he saw and took advantage of opportunities offered him. He does not feel that he planned or plotted his career, but he does believe that when doors were opened to him, he walked through. I asked Joseph how he views the obviously interesting and illustrious career path he had taken—whether he found it fulfilling. "I guess so," he responded. "It was useful, and I'm glad I did it. I don't dwell on it. The reason I did it was it was there to do and I could also learn and experiment."

Coming to Age as an ISTP

Joseph, Clark, and other creatively aging ISTPs do love to learn and experiment. They do things because they are interesting and fun, but also because the things matter to them and serve others. Relationship in the later years is often one of the things that matter greatly. Relationship may even provide one of the best new learning grounds. Creative ISTPs coming to age speak of wanting to help their friends, spend time with their families, and be more accepting of people in general. Clark talks of wanting more time with his grown children.

> *A man I know has a son who gave him a set of golf clubs for a gift.*
> *The son then asked my friend when they could play, and my friend*
> *told me that he thought, with luck, in about two years. This man was*
> *in an important business undertaking that was to last two years, and*
> *only then would he be free for his son. I thought, how sad.*

I asked these active, no-nonsense people how they have changed over the years. "I guess you could say I'm a little softer around the edges," responds Clark.

> *I've become more tolerant and sensitive to shortcomings. I can*
> *sometimes say, Maybe it wasn't their fault. Or if it was their fault,*
> *then it is really a shame. For example, I had a high school classmate*
> *who has recently gotten into trouble with the law. He was an arro-*
> *gant guy in high school, and at forty I would have just dismissed his*
> *troubles without any feeling about him whatsoever. Now I do feel*
> *it's sad. I wonder what happened to him and what caused him to*
> *get in this mess.*

Another ISTP I spoke to, a woman coming to age creatively, also softened a little around the edges. She spoke of an early life acquaintance who had encountered a lot of difficulties.

There was a time when I would have heard her tragic story and said, "I'm sorry, but life is tough. You have to get on with it." Now I think I would say something like, "I wonder how this all happened?" or "How might you be able to handle this now?" This is different for me.

Joseph, while resisting the idea that he has tried to change himself ("Some people just worry about things that it makes no sense to worry about—like changing themselves—although I guess it makes sense to them"), speaks about changes from a type development perspective:

I use my Intuition more. It helps me open up when I take advantage of my opposite type preferences, but it's unpleasant and I like to go back to my own preferences. It's like a rubber band. When I stretch from Sensing to Intuition I feel under tension, and when I go back to Sensing I feel good. I've never been and don't want to be an Intuitive person. But I am more pliable now.

When asked if they have anything they wish to pass on to the next generation, these self-sufficient people talked about balance, about being kind, and about climbing your mountains—but one step at a time. Clark refers to the "monkey principle"—"Don't let go of one limb until you catch the next one."

These present-oriented, practical folks do not talk a great deal about death. When asked about the end of life, almost without exception they responded "Death just is" and then expressed some hope that dying not be a prolonged experience. Most have quite a lot left to do before they seem to need to contemplate the end of life. Or perhaps inquiries about death are just more silly questions.

MARY BETH AND MELISSA—ESTJs

Mary Beth, Age 71

Mary Beth, an athletic-looking seventy-one-year-old woman, is a teacher of religious ethics and an ESTJ. There is a cheerful playfulness as well as a gracious sense of acceptance that marks her life. A growing acceptance of views other than her own, as well as a commitment to her own views, has marked her coming to age. Her humor and optimism, even in the face of some physical diminishment, make her a role model for others and a delight to interview. She sat in her favorite rocking chair across the room from me, surrounded by her many books and several manuscripts she was in the process of writing. Because it was summer break she was not traveling, which her national reputation sometimes requires, and she was not teaching her graduate students, which keeps her occupied full time during the academic year. It appears that she is truly enjoying her life. Although she had several advanced educational degrees and considerable career accomplishments, her conversation bubbled and flowed in a direct and almost folksy manner, without a trace of pretentiousness.

> *I am sunny and optimistic, I guess. Life is good! I do have some aches and pains. Besides a hurting shoulder, I also have some eye problems and can't hear as well as I once did—or jog for that matter. But I can walk, and I do love to walk and take in the beauty of nature. And I'm learning to rely some on tapes and CDs to save my eyes, for reading is so important to me. When the senses start failing, that can hem you in, but you keep doing what you can. You just have to learn to operate in a more constricted sense.*
>
> *I do have some anxiety about the breakdown in my health, of course. Health breakdown is much more frightening than death. Dying is going to be a new discovery. I have a lot of curiosity, and at death we'll get better answers at the great alumni meeting in the sky. That's exciting, but none of us wants to be a burden in this life, and we do wonder about debilitation. Society is not always caring, and nuclear families are overextended. Helplessness and lingering are too hard to contemplate. This life is wonderful. I love to eat, to hike, and to just observe the absolute beauty of creation. I don't want to leave.*

Gratitude marks her conversation, as it also often marks the conversation of other STJs, even as she acknowledges her own efforts as well. She talks about how privileged she has been and how privilege invites generosity.

> *I teach ethics, and I don't teach that it is about law and obligation. Ethics is about gratitude. I do what I do out of gratitude. We're receptors of such grace that what we do is in response to that. I'm so blessed and I give back because of that.*

> *"I've made choices but God wove the wonderful pattern."*

Optimistic as she generally is, she does not underestimate the difficulties of aging. She acknowledges that aging can be difficult and thinks if we can "get ready"—particularly by good financial planning and preparing for role changes—we can better survive the losses of aging. In her own case, she has no plans to give up her work—but rather to simply find a bigger classroom, meaning she'll travel to teach and continue to write once she is no longer teaching full time and "tied to a clock."

She talked of passion and about how it changes its expression. She talked about how the changing tides of culture have invited her to see her passion in a broader context.

> *I'm a feminist. It is my passion, and it is a consistent as well as a changing theme, throughout my life. In the fifties, I was working for racial harmony in the Deep South. In the sixties, it was the civil rights movement. Then in the seventies, it was the women's movement, and then the environmental movement, and now it is homosexual advocacy. I'm an activist and I care deeply. You've got to change structures. To change individuals isn't enough. We are shaped by the society we live in. What underlies this activism in its various forms is, however, very consistent. It is my belief that God wants everyone to have opportunity to be fully human. I don't know where all this passion and activism came from—maybe from God.*
>
> *I was in college during the second world war, and I wanted to do something for peace. I was interested in political science and wanted to work for the State Department, but as a woman that was closed to me at that time. So I went into teaching, preparing people to work in the church, and I work for peace, and for justice, too. I've made choices but God wove the wonderful pattern. God's hand is there and I'm still challenging people to see what He is doing and join Him.*

Melissa, Age 94

Melissa, at ninety-four, is the oldest person I interviewed. Her psychological type is ESTJ. Having lived through the Great Depression, Melissa understands the importance of sound financial planning, but of generosity as well.

You find out what's going on from one year to the next, but you do have to prepare for being old. If you don't, it will be a sad time. And you prepare by saving money. If you don't put it away when you can make it, you can't put it away when you don't have it. Put away half of what comes in and you'll never be hungry. When I was working, I got paid on Friday nights, and the first place I went on Monday mornings was the bank. I've been able to take care of myself, and to lend out and help folks, too. No one else is going to help you out with money unless they have to.

Melissa lives a more restricted life than most people I interviewed due to her age and to the fact that she is dependent on family for her mobility. She has not, however, retired from life.

I visited her in the home of her daughter where she is currently living. Her family had suggested that I interview her, feeling that she exemplifies the creative aging process for them and for her entire community. It is obvious that she does serve as a role model for them, and she has for years been closely involved with her children's families, even taking family vacations with them. She is known as a vivacious, humorous, and very strong woman. Her family admires her courage and strength, and she works hard to live up to their expectation. At thirty-five, she was left with two children, and her current strength may have grown primarily from that time. Finding herself left alone, she went to work and took in boarders and sewing to supplement her income and raise her children. She told me proudly that she not only had raised her children, but had "paid for her home and several cars as well."

> **"I haven't retired from life and I keep up with everyone and what's going on."**

You must have faith in yourself and your fellow man. There have been times when life was tough and I didn't know if I could do it, but you can if you have to. The good Lord looked after me, but I did it. When you have it to do, you just do it. We're so lucky to have family and friends. We must live a good life and be good to our neighbors, for without good friends you're lost. This came from my family. I was the ninth of ten children and we helped each other— and others outside the family who were in need. I still push myself. I haven't retired from life and I keep up with everyone and what's going on. When you have each other, no one can take that from you.

Coming to Age as an ESTJ

These strong, vital, concerned ESTJ women have found that over the years they have become more patient, more understanding, and a little more gracious. Mary Beth said she "knew about these traits early, but living filled them in. I got so I could live them out—sometimes." The community, she said, taught her, and she is grateful to the community.

I'm more patient now when things go wrong and with [laughing]
"idiots who can't see it my way." I still get angry with people who
espouse injustice; but I've been given insight, and I think, maybe
those people have had different experiences and can't be where I am.
For example, I know and care deeply for some homosexual people.
I know these people personally and care greatly for them. Others
who haven't had this experience often see homosexuals just as a
group, and often as a group to be feared. It is my awareness that it is
a person's experiences that allow him or her to be more patient,
understanding, and gracious that has deepened over the years.

Mary Beth says the most significant and freeing gift for herself, and perhaps for others as well, has been her growing and deepening conviction that her "call is not to bring an end to every injustice, but simply to serve faithfully.... It may be just this attitude that underlies the patience, understanding, gratitude, and graciousness that can characterize those aging creatively."

Relationships are important to these ESTJ women, especially relationships that nurture the next generation. These responsible, conscientious people, unlike some others, are not likely to say "I don't give advice" or "Let them find their own way." ESTJs, along with other SJs, feel it is their responsibility to advise and warn younger folks, although they are quick to admit that they may not be heard. One ESTJ man said to me, "The younger folks probably won't listen, but tell them what they need to know anyway. Just don't tell them over and over." And another person said, "Shout down the halls of time to those coming behind you. They may not hear, but you'll know you did what you could. You tried, and that's your part."

The relationship and responsibility to those who will follow is important, but so is the relationship with one's peers. Mary Beth, a never-married woman, speaks of relationship with a group of women friends. It is relationship centered in deep understanding and built on history, commitment, honesty, and care. "I should tell you about the Fried Chicken Society," she began.

The Fried Chicken Society is four women, and sometimes a few more, who have met every Saturday evening for about twenty-five years. We get together and bring a sandwich now, since you can't eat fried chicken anymore with all this health concern around. I care deeply about these women, and I just make my plans to be there with them. We share whatever is going on in our lives and whatever is bothering us as well. We call each other and check up on each other. Recently I went out to make a speech and the next day back I get a telephone call from one of the Fried Chicken members. "Were you brilliant?" she asked.

BILL AND KARLA—ESTPs

Bill, Age 61

Bill is a retired military officer who now does some part-time consulting and spends a large portion of his work time in a prison ministry program. His psychological type is ESTP. Bill has been married for thirty-six years and is father to three grown children. At sixty-one, Bill feels he has found a sense of commitment and fulfillment that enriches his life and makes "sixty better than fifty or forty."

Bill says his military career "just happened." He had grown up knowing that after college a young male would do his military service, and so one day he "was walking with a friend through the student union at his college, noticed a military recruiter, and signed on" with the intent to just "do his military duty" and then go to seminary. However, he liked the style of the military—the challenges and the opportunity for learning and travel. He even liked moving from one place to another. He stayed twenty-eight years and found it meaningful—especially the pride he felt when he was being "the best he could be." The military style of concise, accurate, and nonambiguous communicating also appealed to him.

> *"I don't spend much time worrying. It's not productive."*

Bill didn't go to seminary because he wasn't ready "to take the vow of poverty" and because he didn't feel an "authentic call" at that time that a "fundamental Christian such as he" should feel. Now, however, in semiretirement, he spends three days each week on prison ministry and manages the structure that administers the ministry. It adds meaning to his life.

> *I've always been involved in church—Bible study, prayer, mowing the grass—and I've always asked what the Lord wants me to do. I hoped He might want me to be the next Billy Graham, but instead I think he wants me to work in the prisons. . . . Somehow—I don't remember how—I found out about a chaplaincy program for service in local jails. There are no paid chaplains there, so I went to school to become a chaplain. I do worship services and chaplaincy, and these are two different things. When we lead worship we have a "discussion"—although people say when I lead discussion I preach a little sermon. In chaplaincy we listen. I do tend to preach little sermons, but I can just listen, too. Just listening is often all you can do.*

I say this is quite a commitment, these two or three days each week in prison ministry and administrative work to support the effort as well. However, *commitment* is not a good choice of word for Sensing Thinking people.

> *It's an opportunity and a blessing for me. I'm thankful for the opportunity, though not for the committee meetings. I don't want to sit around and talk about the problems. I want to do something about them. I don't know why I have been given this time and adequate finances to be able to do this work.*

Bill, as he looked back upon his life, said that he believes he was not sensitive enough earlier about how disruptive his military lifestyle—which he enjoyed—was for the others in his family. He is pleased to have lived for a number of years since retirement in his present home, for it allows his wife the geographic stability that she had not had previously. He says he might redo some of his parenting, too, but he isn't worried a great deal about it. "I don't spend much time worrying. It's not productive," he tells me. And, "If parents don't regret some things, they're out of touch."

Karla, Age 58

Karla, at fifty-eight, was the youngest person I interviewed. Her psychological type is ESTP. Her earlier life, like that of Bill and of many other ESPs, was not "chosen" in the usual sense of "planned." But her choices are now made with considerable awareness. She has assessed her situation realistically, and now is committed to providing for her financial security and for the relationship and home she has chosen and cares greatly for.

Karla met me at the front door of the large, beautifully landscaped home she had built with a close friend whom she refers to as her chosen (not biological) sister. She spoke to me about working in several Protestant churches as a director of Christian education. In fact, it was in one of her churches that she met the woman who became her housemate after the deaths of Karla's father and the woman's mother a few weeks apart. They knew they had similar values and family backgrounds, and they decided to pool their resources to provide a larger and more attractive living space than they could have otherwise afforded. It was obvious that Karla had committed to this home and the relationship with the woman she called sister, as well as to providing for her own retirement.

"How did you come to this house?" I asked. "We were just out driving around and saw the houses being built in this neighborhood. It made sense to buy a partially completed house and finish it," she answered, laughing as she recognized the casual way they found the house as having much in common with her method of choosing careers.

> I thought God wanted me to be a missionary, so I got a master's degree in rural sociology called Church and Community. But I didn't become a missionary. I went to work for a church instead. I decided I'd better get another degree, and I got one in Christian education. I enjoyed my decade of work in churches. The work was primarily with youth, and I like kids. The problem was I didn't have any benefits. I was rich with friends and experiences, and I wouldn't take ten million dollars for that, but I'm paying every day for it now. One day I realized I didn't want to spend the end of my life on welfare. I'd made a comment to a friend earlier that when I got too old to run over sand dunes and hop on hayride trucks with the kids, I would like to work with the aging population. I went to work for a social services department licensing homes for adults and I liked it, but it didn't really use my training. Then I was switched over to the social services child care area, and I developed policies and standards. I hadn't planned this. Really I had planned to go in another direction, but I liked the child care area. This position, however, got dropped, and I ended up doing policy work for

*the adult care homes for a while until a training position opened in
the social services department, where I got to do team building and
such. I had been waiting for that. It used my training at last. One
door slams and two or three open. I never plotted and planned
where I would be in two or three years. I always liked where I was.*

This optimistic, take-life-as-it-comes attitude applies to relationships
as well as to work. The direct, down-to-earth ESTPs appreciate straightforward, concise interactions and are bothered by "whining" and people
who "sit around and feel sorry for themselves." Karla doesn't know how
she could have lived without her straight-shooting, honest father, although
she has to struggle with a brother whose manner is quite different.

> "I never plotted and
> planned where I would be
> in two or three years. I
> always liked where I was."

Developing spaciousness of personality is
often encouraged for ESTPs, as for many
others, when troublesome relationships
have to be worked through. True spaciousness of personality for the no-nonsense
ESTPs can occur when they are "big enough" to appreciate that which is
truly different in other people. Karla's family has presented her with
relationship challenges as well as comfort. She is open to learning from
these, and the learnings may continue for some time.

*Dad and I had a unique and special relationship. He had been an
athlete, and he was a sportsman who hunted and fished. Some girls
take their questions to their mothers, but I took mine to him. There
was nothing my dad and I and God couldn't handle. Now, I guess,
since he's gone, it's up to God and me. With Dad, right was right
and wrong was wrong, but he could apologize. He may have had
only a seventh-grade education, but he had integrity.*

Karla spoke of her brother and her troubled relationship with him. As
I listened, I reflected on the continuing struggles that those of us coming
to age have even as we assert, as Karla does, that we are basically content
and living just as we wish to live. She talked of how she had stayed awake
at night worrying about this relationship, how she had prayed and talked
to people about it. Withholding behavior is difficult for Karla and for
others as well. Being blocked from being able to act when action is
called for is also a problem for her. Karla and other ESTPs have difficulty relating to people they feel are not honest, open, and direct. She

has little tolerance for those who don't take responsibility for the "hard things," and she is aware that some people find her impatient and insensitive. But Karla is trying. She related a three-and-a-half-hour conversation she had had with her brother under a tree at their mother's home in which she had said, "I am sorry. It was half my fault; no, it was three-fourths my fault; no, it was all my fault. Can't you forgive me so we can move on?" She relates that she said that four times.

Karla reports that things are now "on the mend." In fact, her brother had just called to invite her and their sister to join him for a holiday.

Coming to Age as an ESTP

While worrying about and massaging relationships can seem nonproductive and a waste of time to the ESTPs, they often show great care in relationships through direct, practical effort. Bill talks about helping out an eighty-six-year-old woman who lives alone several states away, and who is dying.

> *She never married and has no relatives, and she has made all the arrangements for after her death. She knows she is going to God, but it's not good to die like this. I'm going to see her four times a year now and help her out with things. When she dies, I'll claim the body and I'll go with her body and see that she has a service and is buried well. That's what I can do.*

Karla hopes that when she's retired, she will have time to work in a home for elderly folks, "washing hair and cutting toenails." She hopes that when she dies, she'll be remembered as "fun loving" and as "one who kept going till the end, doing what she could while it mattered." She thinks that perhaps her epitaph could read, "She has done what she could." Karla says she is doing what she can now, and she is not waiting to "send flowers to folks when they can't smell."

The confident, straightforward, action-oriented Bill and Karla do what they can. Worries are not excessive, although one common concern is how to accommodate declining health and limitations. They haven't yet found an answer—perhaps because it hasn't happened yet—but they are aware that something beyond physical exercise may be needed to cope in later life. They are realists and they don't expect a smooth road.

Many coming to age ESTPs feel that things are as they are and one deals with that fact. "I would change almost nothing about my life," says Bill.

If someone twenty years ago had told me that I would like sixty better than fifty, I wouldn't have believed it. Maybe it isn't true for everyone, but, fortunately, I'm physically able and it is true for me. My eyes and memory are not quite as good, but I adjust. I've always been connected to God, though distracted in the heavy career parts of my life. He didn't promise us a rose garden. Life isn't perfect.

I feel fortunate that my life has been full and rewarding. I've had accomplishments, although no one is building a statue to commemorate my life—at least that I know of. It would have been nice to have been a general, but that is very political and I preferred to be honest and sincere—and to be friends with the people I liked rather than those I was supposed to be friends with.

I adjust to what is in the neighborhood of possibility. If I can't do something, I accept it or make some change. I couldn't play a sport on the high school team, so I played on the church team. I now run for enjoyment, not for competition. Some people say this attitude is rationalizing, but I don't think so. I don't talk on and on about what I can't do, I just go find what I can do. I'm contented. I understand what life is about from my experience—not from some outside source. I know what is important and what's not. My health and my family's health and our financial security are important.

Bill speaks of death as he speaks of life. He accepts that "whatever will be, will be" with typical ESTP philosophy and humor, and talks about his final wishes.

There is a bike trail here that runs over some paved-over railroad tracks, and I do a lot of running and biking there. I want my family to cremate my body and take my biking and hiking friends to this place where we've had so much fun and spread my ashes on that trail. They can all have a Chardonnay or a beer and enjoy themselves. And I want my children to throw out wildflower seeds. Then each spring they can go there, see the flowers blooming, and say, "There's my blooming dad." I don't want my death to be a burden. I've lived the way I wanted to. I've been blessed.

BOB AND JAMES—ISTJs

Bob, Age 61

Bob is a sixty-one-year-old Episcopal priest whose psychological type is ISTJ. He is married and has three grown children. He talked of the pain and shared suffering that his family has endured and what gifts these difficulties have brought. His older son had been diagnosed with AIDS eleven years earlier, and this sad fact had taught him a great deal about the problem of stereotyping. "It is no longer 'those homosexuals' but 'my son, the homosexual.' I don't have to categorize people. I really can take them as they are, and it has not always been this way," he said. His other children had not escaped difficulty, either. Divorce, rape, and illness had touched their lives. However, if all these things had not happened, painful as they certainly were, he felt he might still be living inside himself without intimate relationships. "My life has pulled me out and allowed me to form relationships and to love," he said. Life's pulling out has not been easy for Bob, as it is not for most people. But in true ISTJ style, when he sees what needs to be done, he steps forth to do it, sparing no effort.

> *"My life has pulled me out and allowed me to form relationships and to love."*

Bob described his earlier life as dominated by "a need to carve out a space" for himself. Now he wonders "what success is" and even if he would know it if he saw it.

> Success isn't what happens outside, but coming to know Bob and being happy in spite of external life circumstances. I'm blessed with my work and blessed to be able to live in a rural, natural place. My self-discovery will continue right on. When life calls we must risk and live life—whatever it brings. In honestly living you find life.

He wonders what would have happened had he not risked, and he is glad he took some risks, but they were difficult for him. He has had to let go over and over, and not without anxiety. He tells me an amusing story about his recent move to a new house.

> Each time we went from our old house to the new house we were building, we would take a trailerload of possessions. One day my wife put her clothes in the trailer, and then she put my clothes in.

I took mine out and put them back in the closet. I wasn't quite ready for this change; things were moving too fast. Then she moved the washing machine out and I had no choice but to follow with my clothes.

James, Age 84

James is an eighty-four-year-old man who lives in a retirement center. His psychological type is also ISTJ. "I didn't know I was getting old until my wife died," he began. James had been a successful student and had attended a military college. When he graduated in the midst of the Great Depression, he found it difficult to secure a job. Eventually he did secure one, in the financial world. In order to supplement his income, he began to teach at night. "I had a good job offer to work for a public utility, but I had signed on to teach so I had to teach." This was to lead him eventually, but not immediately, into a career in teaching and school administration. More immediately, all was interrupted by World War II, which sent him to the Pacific and to Europe.

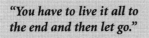

"You have to live it all to the end and then let go."

Things just happen. You have to be lucky. I made captain and all that stuff in the army, but I take no credit. People take care of you. I had a good family and a happy childhood, and I got good military assignments. I was lucky. Some people got killed.

James talks about the changes he experienced in coming to age. There is an easing of judgment toward himself and others.

Judgment is fallible. You hope you can make the right decisions, but you learn you can live with the wrong ones. When I have a decision to make I ponder it in my head, but pondering isn't enough. You have to act. You know what you're supposed to do by living it. You learn from mistakes. I've been called a "worry wart." I want to tell younger people not *to worry, but I also want to tell them* to *worry. You have to live it all. You have to live it all to the end and then let it go. Life comes together. You may not understand it, but you accept it.*

Coming to Age as an ISTJ

Things do tend, for the successfully aging ISTJs, to move toward realization that much of life is bigger and more mysterious than expected and to move toward "the way of the heart." But the way is still the grounded way. Integrity requires that the ISTJ answer carefully and honestly. Abstractions that do not carry meaning for them are not accepted.

About a year ago, with the wear of time and hard work taking a toll, Bob found he was thinking of heading for retirement as soon as it was feasible, although the thought came to him, he soberly recalled, that his father and grandfather had both died within a year of their own retirements. A dream broke in.

> I'm back at one of the parishes I formerly served. It is a large church, and I am this day's celebrant for the main service. I am vested, but instead of going to the altar I go, in the dream, out the church door. I'm a few blocks from the church in the city, and there is a round circle with a water fountain in the middle. People are waiting for the Eucharist and, as I approach the fountain, I see under the water the chalice, the bread, and a candle. I start to light the candle underwater, and there is a shift in the dream. I'm now away from the circle and the fountain trying to find my way back to celebrate Eucharist.

He went on to say that he does not know what the dream means. What is clear, however, is that his energy is drawing him not toward retirement but toward the excitement of what is unfolding. It isn't "renewal, but rather transformation," he says, and he knows his ministry, whatever form it takes, will be more "inclusive and more out there." It will be "the way of the heart." This is enough to know, for the rest will unfold.

CONCLUSION

So, generally, how have these creative people changed? How are they different in their coming to age period from the way they were earlier in their lives? What are the unexpected joys of the Sensing Thinking

people in the later years? I suggest they are graciousness and spaciousness. These creative people coming to age expand and deepen their
ways of seeing and stretch their hearts.

Empathy in relationships for the Sensing Thinking people, it
seems, develops with the passage of time. And there is always the desire
for fun-loving relationships—sometimes the desire for a playmate. One
man spoke of his disappointment when his wife's interests took a turn
toward returning to school and he no longer had anyone "to play with."
And one daughter spoke movingly of a playfulness, gentleness, and joy
that she saw in her Sensing Thinking father only near the end of his life.

> I watched my father play with my children. My important, hard-
> working, lawyer father was sitting on the floor in an old red
> bathrobe playing with my sons and their toys. I never knew he
> could be so gentle, so accepting, so relaxed, and so playful. I was
> a bit sad I had never known as his child that he could really be
> so much fun and that he could have so much fun.

Sensing Thinking people coming to age more comfortably embrace
different views and multiple options. They lessen their judgment and make
room for others, and for reflection, ambiguity, and complexity. They
more easily recognize the abundance of what they have been given—
even sometimes in a spiritual sense—and they respond out of gratitude, especially toward their families. Clark (ISTP) wants to rearrange
the blocks of his life to find more time for family. Karla (ESTP) has
devoted a lot of her fifties to building a life with her chosen sister. Bob
(ISTJ) also talks of what he has received from his family. "Family was the
crucible," he says. "Who I am at this moment is because of my experiences with my family. When my children suffer, my heart is touched."

CHAPTER 6

CONNECTEDNESS AND RELATEDNESS

*There are many truths of which the full
meaning cannot be realized until personal
experience has brought it home.*

—John Stuart Mill

NT True connection and relatedness are often unexpected joys of the later years for these independent, autonomous people who value competency, intellect, will, and reason—characteristics associated with preferences for Intuition and Thinking. As they age, these people feel increasingly connected to their true selves and to their softer emotions, and are able to find more self-acceptance and self-love. Others are able to feel more connected to them as well. For the person who prefers Intuition and Thinking, creatively coming to age means an increasing delight in the laying down of armor, even as highly valued individuality is preserved.

*T*he well-developed Intuitive Thinking types (INTP, ENTP, INTJ, ENTJ) have been described as visionary, creative, intellectual, logical, analytical, and abstract. They value knowledge and like to focus on the big picture and on the future. They derive pleasure from creating new models, whether they be new visions for organizations and groups (ENTP), new models for organizing companies and groups (ENTJ and INTJ), or organizing ideas and concepts (INTP). Interviews with them are marked by concentration and directness, and by the logic and analysis characteristic of Thinking types, whether it be the generally accepted logic and analysis of the Extraverts or the highly subjective and very precise logic and analysis of the Introverts. They value fairness and are driven by a desire for competency. They make many demands on themselves and others—perhaps too many demands.

As children, Intuitive Thinking people are often curious, and they ask hard questions. If they are fortunate, they may find themselves respected by their parents and teachers for their inquisitiveness and their logical/analytical approach. Or they may find themselves criticized by parents and teachers for their lack of sensitivity, and sometimes for their lack of respect for authority as well.

At midlife, they may find that their search for knowledge, as important as it is, has taken them about as far as it can, and that their drive for excellence is tiring them out. They often discover that they feel isolated, burdened, and overwhelmed with too many demands. Sometimes they find that they are having difficulty with relationships at work and in their personal lives as well. Questions about how to connect more fully with themselves and others without "selling out," "becoming a wimp," or "compromising one's standards"

> *As they age, they find they are not as likely to be burdened and held back by a fear of vulnerability or of looking foolish.*

become important. The relationship style they seek is not the seeking, sharing Intuitive Feeling style, and it is certainly not the hands-on, caregiving, serving Sensing Feeling style. Rather, it is often relationship built on communication with others and with mentoring and educating the next generation. It seems that often there can be a great sense of meaning for the Intuitive Thinking person who can find a way to communicate and pass on to others what he or she has come to know.

As they age, Intuitive Thinking people often feel more connected and related to others. One man said, "I know much more than I need to know. I'm now surprised by the passion I have toward people. I care deeply about them, and I want them to care about me. This surprises and frightens me, for it isn't as comfortable as cognitive things."

As these competent, independent people age, they find they are not as likely to be burdened and held back by a fear of vulnerability or of looking foolish. And as they can more easily trust, they find that they can put down some of their own armor, which isolates and protects them from others. One woman talked about trust in this way:

I was almost fifty when I learned I could trust the universe a little— not just myself. With that awareness, I was able to lay down some of my armor. There's plenty that is wrong with the world, and I'll fight these things, but I'm not angry now. I'm not burdened as I was.

They are often surprised and delighted to find themselves more connected to themselves as well. They find that they can come to accept themselves, and even love themselves, limitations and all. They can come to more easily accept and appreciate the ordinary in themselves and others. They discover the freedom of not having to always be right even as they continue to protect the truth that they know. "It's about joining the human race as one of them," said one woman.

They don't have to force as many things. One person told me, "I still love to learn and always will, but I'm no longer learning in order to make something happen—yet something often does happen." They don't have to rely as heavily on will and reason. They can free up a lot of energy that previously had been spent persuading—or forcing—people and events to be as they felt they should be. They often find themselves more patient and less driven. As one Intuitive Thinking man coming to age said, "Joy is watching children play. I just stand and watch. I don't do anything and I don't think about what is happening. I don't need anything else. Believe you me, this is different."

As they lessen criticism and the demand for knowledge and competency beyond their capacity to achieve, the Intuitive Thinking people may find, almost without knowing how it happened, that they are less burdened and more free. They may find to their surprise and delight the gifts of connectedness and relatedness that are rarely available to the independent, intellectual Intuitive Thinking younger people.

Connectedness and relatedness for the Intuitive Thinking person is not a sloppy "anything goes" attitude. There is always distinction. It is not sentimental, but it is related to the softer emotions and to a more yielding nature. It is an attitude of relatedness, compassion, and care based on understanding. They may find themselves experiencing what Henry Nouwen calls " humor with a soft smile." They may look at the world with the detachment and wisdom that come with age, but with concern and care as well.

Relatedness often allows the tough mind of the Intuitive Thinking person to be tempered by connection with the heart and with personal experience. These people creatively coming to age may find themselves listening gently to their inner selves and finding appreciation and devotion to that which they hear and feel. They see some of their own limitations and accept them rather than struggling to correct or hide them. They find their heads informed by "parts of their bodies below the neck."

Connectedness is that which allows these visionary people to relate the general to the specific and the abstract to the personal. They can connect their global concerns to available mundane tasks and discover great pleasure in interacting with the joys and pains of the immediate, ordinary world and its ordinary people. Others may experience them as more relational while also experiencing them as "sagelike." When the Intuitive Thinking person is connected and related, others see her or his knowledge as wisdom and feel more cherished and less judged when in her or his presence. They sense a new kind of patience and receptivity and tenderness.

ELLEN AND MARTHA—INTPs

Service is not usually a word chosen by younger Intuitive Thinking people when they talk of what gives them pleasure. Their autonomous and independent nature and their gifts with conceptualizing and imagining can sometimes disconnect these people from opportunities for one-on-one intimacy and from everyday opportunities to serve as well, and finding a desire for service in later years is often surprising to them.

Now come and meet some creative Intuitive Thinking people who are coming to age.

Ellen, Age 65
Meet Ellen, whose work and passion is art, and who finds herself, at sixty-five, surprised by a desire to be of service. Her psychological type is INTP. She is a divorced mother living alone, and she is happy. "Life is terrific,

and I love my freedom," she tells me as we sit down amidst her vibrant paintings and her thriving houseplants. Around her unusual home are woods and an assortment of wildlife. "I love this place I live in," she tells me. "You can hardly drag me from here." I

"Life is terrific, and I love my freedom."

can understand that. The space seems to fit her. It is complex without the neat boundaries of city lots, and it has ample space for digging, for meditating, and for dreaming.

At the time of the interview she felt pushed, for she was preparing to show her work. But then, she is usually pushed, for she works hard. "I have a regular job," she told me. "I go to my studio in the morning and I work until evening. My time off is nights and weekends like anyone else who works full time."

She began our interview by telling me that she does not like to generalize about type—or about anything else, for that matter. It is dangerous. She acknowledged that when she thinks of aging, she realizes her body strength has changed and she can't do everything she once did. But she accepts it. "I hate the word *accept,* but I do," she says. "It doesn't make me angry anymore, but I do sigh. I complain, but I really don't want to go back in my life." She says her work is her god—perhaps a false god, and explains.

> *My art makes me feel worthwhile. I don't feel this changing. I want to die with a paintbrush in my hand. I've been told you have to give up that which means most to you, but I can't. You would have to break my arm. I'd rather be miserable in my studio than out having a good time somewhere else. I am conscious of this and don't want it to change. It gives a center to my life and I don't want to lose this passion.*
>
> *When I start a painting, it's like I have a splendid thing by the tail and I'm pulling it out of its hole. It's alive and it wants to be done. Nothing comes close to this high—well sex, maybe, but not quite. Then I use my meticulous, realistic style to say what I need to say. I feel like I'm doing what I'm supposed to be doing in the way I'm supposed to be doing it even if I don't like it. You really put yourself in service of something. If I didn't do the meticulous, realistic work, my painting wouldn't have impact. I want it to have impact.*

Ellen talks about being blocked—when the high of having some splendid thing by the tail is denied. "One day," she related, "I was blocked and I found myself raving at God. That surprised me, for I don't usually acknowledge God." Ellen is a complex woman who understands paradox and is quite aware of herself. She does not like "being used," that is, being in service, but also recognizes there is pleasure as well in "being used." She wants to make an impact, but she wants to be herself. She knows we all need to be recognized for the special, unique human beings we are. When one is in service one is making an impact and one is not being ignored. She relates a little story.

> I remember a time when I was visiting daily in a hospital. Each day I would walk by a room occupied by a woman crying, "Save me, save me." One day I entered and asked her, "What can I do for you?" She gave me her names, again and again. She gave me not one name, but all the names she had ever been called, all her nicknames, her maiden name, her married names. I knew she wanted to be called by name. I knew she thought no one knew her, really, and she wanted them to know her—to call her by name. She wasn't important to anyone, and that is what she wanted to be saved from.

She continued, becoming a bit more personal about her desire to be in service.

> In the last five years or so I've come to see my work differently. I've always feared psychological inflation, feeling too self-important. But my work isn't about that. It is in service. This puts it into the great pool of creative activity. It takes it out of the personal and puts it in the pool of creative activity with all the rest of creative activity such as writing, gardening, bricklaying, or whatever. It doesn't matter what the creative expression is. All add to the worth of the world.

Martha, Age 68

Martha, whose psychological type is also INTP, is a very different person from Ellen, but also a person of great passion. Her passion is to understand cultural and racial differences. Her concern is a global concern, "as is typical of her typology," she said, but it is grounded in the everyday tasks of her work. Through teaching the skills of creative thinking, she wants to help young people see their immediate experience as a part of something much bigger and to see the much bigger concerns related to their everyday experience. She feels grateful and fulfilled to be able to speak up about what she believes in and to be connected to the next generation.

Martha was described by an acquaintance as "born to the manor." She is from a large city in the Northeast, and she grew up with many opportunities—especially educational opportunities. She appreciates her classical liberal arts education and her teachers' emphasis on the importance of a democratic society. She has an acute desire to be a "universal human being, not a member of some small group," and recognizes the advantages and disadvantages of her "WASP upbringing." In her early years, she attended youth conferences to meet different kinds of people and further extend her horizons. And she has had a particular concern for the struggle of the African Americans in this country. She married a man destined for corporate leadership, which destined her for the corporate wife role. After forty-five years of marriage and raising a large family, she is living her life the way she wants to. In many ways, she can be seen as a model of creative aging.

> *"I like to teach young folks to think for themselves, to see beyond the immediate but also to make relationship to the immediate."*

> *Early in our marriage, my husband and I lived in the Middle East. I often ask myself if I learned more from my education or from my experiences. My education taught me a lot about responsible citizenship and the importance of maintaining democracy, and the experience of living in the Middle East taught me so much about differences. After that time abroad, we returned and lived in several different places in the States—including a small farm town where life was about as different from my upbringing as that in the Middle East had been. I've long been interested in the civil rights movement. I know there are racial problems, but there are also cultural problems. Being in a foreign culture taught me to try to learn about other people and their ways before expecting them to learn who I am.*
>
> *While raising our five children, I taught science part time, and was particularly involved in racial issues in the schools. I got interested in creative thinking, and I taught courses in it for an urban school gifted program. In my fifties, I earned a Ph.D. in critical creative thinking, and about a decade ago I formed the nonprofit*

company that I work in now. In our company, we work to encour-
age critical creative thinking. There is a lot of discussion about cre-
ative thinking improving a democratic society—but not a lot being
done about it. We offer CEU courses; I teach a course in college,
and we work with faculties trying to restructure schools.

Martha's life is about improving people's understanding of cultural
and personal differences. Her concerns at the age of sixty-eight are global
ones. "War is insane, illogical, and idiotic," she says. She copes with
these feelings by working with younger generations. It is here she finds
joy and meaning.

I like to teach the young folks to think for themselves, to see beyond
the immediate but also to make relationship to the immediate. For
example, I was teaching a class and I showed a map of the United
States on which active Nazi groups had been identified. This was
strange to a lot of the students to think of active Nazi groups in this
country, but one girl spoke up and told of one of her former schools
where a Nazi group had tried to have all the black students dismissed.
Talking about that girl's situation really brought it home for the stu-
dents, and they talked about how they could change things. I'm glad I
can teach creative thinking. I'm glad I can speak up when it is appro-
priate, and I feel fortunate to have access to the younger generations.

Martha also talked about her experience as a corporate wife and
about the changes in role expectations that occurred in her generation.

I didn't have a lot of success with social life as a corporate wife.
Most of the many dinner parties I attended were boring, and at
times I wanted to kick a few shins. But I got out of the WASP circle
because I was teaching and my colleagues were different from the
dinner party group. In some ways, I was a little problem for my
husband, but this had a good outcome, too. Because of his position
and having me for a wife, he became a leader in encouraging men
to relieve their wives of having to be the "corporate wife." My gen-
eration is a swing group, you know. We were taught the thing to do
was to fill the station wagon with children, and when we did that
we were told that was not the thing to do. I've paid a price. I was a
heavy smoker and drinker, and I think that came from stress and
from picking up a lot of negative vibes about myself .

Coming to Age as an INTP

Ellen and Martha and others coming to age find the global most satis-fying when linked to the particular of each day, whether this be a stu-dent, a painting, or some ordinary life event. They find joy in commu-nicating and making a difference.

Martha learned to accept herself and found that knowledge was the way to acceptance. She had learned about accepting others through her education and through her experience of living in other cultures. She learned about accepting herself through the MBTI, through therapy, and through her critical thinking skills.

> I've come to know that to be a female INTP is to almost guarantee a sense of isolation. It helps when I'm angry to look at what's happen-ing, and the MBTI and critical thinking have helped me with this. I can depersonalize behavior and I can know I'm not crazy. I don't have to be angry or feel so isolated when I understand what's going on.

Ellen told of a retreat experience where she, too, came to accept herself —limitations and all—and the sense of freedom that can come from this.

> At a retreat we were to do some free movement. I couldn't do it. Then one morning, when no one was looking, I did it. I just moved and it felt marvelous. Tears started and they just wouldn't stop. The retreat was safe, and no one, thank heavens, touched me or said, "It's okay." The weight of the world was gone. It was like the free-dom of being whole, but not perfect. I've hurt people and that's part of my wholeness. I felt free as hell.

How do these intellectually curious people who value honesty and integrity integrate a sense of purpose in their lives as they come to age? How do they speak of spiritual matters and of the final leaving of life? As one might expect, they speak with honesty and authenticity and a lack of conventionality. Ellen tells this story:

> One night, when my teenage son was out with the car long after the time I had expected him home and I was really worried, I found I could pray. I didn't say "take care of him," but rather I said "please be with him." It was like shooting an arrow and letting it go. God is whoever or whatever I say please to, and that is all I want to know.

I don't need to know more. God for me is not what I was taught in church. A limited God isn't worth believing in. God is way beyond our ideas of good and evil. I hope I never hear another sermon. As for death, sometimes I look forward to it, for life can be hard just as it can be wonderful. I don't fear death, but I choose life.

Martha, whose life theme is appreciation of cultural diversity, shares her views about God and about death:

The way I see it is that God is spoken in many tongues and the right way to speak may still be to be discovered. Let's don't argue about who is right about God. None of us knows. . . .

Humans arrange things, but we didn't invent anything. Yet not having invented anything, it is amazing what we've done. I personally don't think it is very important what I'm remembered for. After I'm gone, it's someone else's business.

JIM AND SYLVIA—INTJs

Jim, Age 74

Jim is a seventy-four-year-old INTJ who has spent a lot of his life working for others, if not serving others, as a business executive, a husband, and a father. He has played many roles that "make a difference." Now his inner life and his solitude give him great joy.

> **"You can walk sideways, but it tires you out."**

The natural world feeds him, and authenticity and integrity are his prime values.

If people in the community were to be asked to describe Jim, such words as *interesting* and *reserved* would surely be chosen. He is an engineer who took early retirement and spent a large part of his life living in a large log cabin where he cut wood, enjoyed music, and built boats and harpsichords. He is married and the father of three grown children. He loves to take his grandchildren out on his boat and teach them "to throw line, splice, and so forth, so that when they go home they will know that they helped plot the compass course and that they got where they were heading."

Jim began our interview, as did Ellen, by making certain that I knew that type "does not explain everything," that surely with any typology "you will get a wide range of experience." Yet he also felt that type knowledge is a very helpful thing and, in fact, he doesn't know how we could get along without it.

Our conversation quickly moved, as it often does with men, to the area of work—or, in Jim's case, to the joy of being away from work. In retirement, "every morning is like Christmas morning," he began. "When I thought I might retire, I checked out the finances and found it was possible. It was like getting out of school." Every morning he "gets up and gets going." There is sailing to do, community work to help out with, something to be built. "There are things to do each morning, and thank God I have the health to do them."

Perhaps Jim's satisfaction with retirement is due to some degree to the fact that his identity was never tied to his work. He had a successful career as an engineer and worked as a manager of a number of other engineers, but he has never felt that engineering was a "calling" for him. In fact, he remembers a midlife period of real turmoil revolving primarily around career issues.

> You can walk sideways, but it tires you out. I was trying to be what I wasn't, and my way was a twisted and contorted way. I was pushing down my feelings about what I wanted to do and trying to be acceptable. One co-worker once said I was the coldest man he had ever known. I was so hard on myself, and I came across as being hard on him. I wore my armor, but my armor did have a visor and sometimes I could raise the visor. There was someone in there, but you wouldn't often know it. Armor looks good and protects you from perceived threats. I wasn't really an engineer and I wasn't a "nice person," if by nice person you mean pleasant, with good feeling, happy— and phony.

Jim's life did not change suddenly, but it has changed. The phrase "I used to be different, but now I'm the same" is not original, he said, but it is a good expression of what he feels has happened in his life. He explained that he used to be divided—that is, "one thing was going on inside and other people saw something very different." He also hastened to explain that this split between what is really going on and how he allows others to see him is still sometimes present. "Leopards don't change their spots," he said. The time when Jim finds it hardest to be authentic and stay focused is when he is in a social situation in which he wants to make a good impression. This may explain some of the delight he feels when he is alone and doesn't have to "justify himself," go along with others, or disagree and cause them disappointment. "I feel most integrated when I'm alone," says Jim.

Jim talked about the time he has left.

I built a boat between my fortieth and sixtieth years. It took me fourteen years. I would like to do that again because I could make some improvements on it. I won't, though, for I don't have fourteen more years for hard labor. Recently I bought some Florsheim shoes and I realized I won't need to buy any more Florsheim shoes ever again—not ever.

But I did not really hear too much regret in this awareness. He explained that although there are things he just can't have now, there are also many delicious things that he can still enjoy. "I won't write a big book, but I enjoy writing memoirs. The body is slower and sexual arousal takes a little longer, but some people claim that the ninth decade can be the most productive."

Jim and others speak of having to live up to others' expectations or "walking sideways" as being the thing that has held them back. They feel that their natural tendency to be direct, and the fact that they are often perceived as distant, have also sometimes cut them off from others and from themselves. When they become more authentically themselves they like themselves better and they like others better as well.

Sylvia, Age 64

Sylvia is a trim, energetic, attractive, and direct woman of sixty-four years. She is quite knowledgeable about the *Myers-Briggs Type Indicator* (MBTI) personality inventory and sometimes uses it in her work. Her psychological type is INTJ.

Sylvia has been married for forty-five years. She is one of the middle siblings in a family of six children and was born on a small farm. "We were poor, but we didn't know we were poor," she informed me. She described her family as being Sensing types, in MBTI terms, and believes she was the only Intuitive type in the family. She was also the only one to continue her education beyond high school. Her determination was evident. As a young woman, she taught school. She then married, gave birth to three children in three and a half years, earned a master's degree, and "worked hard at being a wife and mother." She explained that these early child-rearing years were difficult. "I tried hard to be what a mother was supposed to be. I kept house and did what my mother had done. I worked hard at keeping it together and staying on top of things." At midlife, with her youngest entering high school, she went back to school to obtain a second master's degree. And although her husband wasn't particularly pleased by that, she felt it was something she needed to do. She felt it was important for her to get up in the morning and get out of the house, and to have her own charge card and bank account.

Sylvia felt that for her, coming to age meant realizing the importance of being able to be herself and to be in relationships that allow her to be relaxed and comfortable, particularly the relationship with her husband.

> *Friends are fun, but I love being with just the two of us. I know nothing about his work, nor he about mine, but we do love music, theater, and travel. We can talk or not talk. We're relaxed and it's comfortable. No big productions. I'm not into big productions now. This became obvious to me this week when in the middle of shampooing the rugs, finding the silver, and unearthing the linen tablecloths for the shower I'm giving next week for a friend's daughter, my husband and I just decided to have a couple over for supper. We had furniture stacked up and a pot of soup on the stove. I got some bread and a dessert out of the freezer, we made a spot to sit down, and we had a wonderful evening. We had lots of soup and we talked and talked. It was comfortable and relaxed.*

For Sylvia, who prefers soup suppers to formal events, spirituality is very important and at times quite problematic. She let her conversation drift, without being asked, to matters of spirit. I felt that this was an important area for her— and one of some considerable pain.

> **"I've had mystical experiences, but I don't like to talk about them. Some things don't need to be explained."**

> *I see God as the Spirit, not Christ the human or Christ the Word. The Spirit resonates. I can't talk much about it, but it's there. I've had mystical experiences, but I don't like to talk about them. Some things don't need to be explained.*

Sylvia talks about the problems at her church, where she has found not only insufficient religious experience, but what feels like rejection.

I go to church regularly. I've worked a lot in the church and served on a lot of committees and boards. I can't say my more mystical experiences have ruined church for me, but I look for more than the church is able to give me. I've tried at church to teach some of the classes I took elsewhere, but they weren't popular. Sometimes we can get a good book discussion going, but often when I put myself up to teach a class that means a lot to me I get so disappointed. I so much want to share, but they don't want it. It feels like rejection to me, not personal rejection of me, but rejection of what really matters to me.

Coming to Age as an INTJ

It seems that coming to age as an INTJ involves being able to tenderly accept oneself. Using their Thinking preference helps INTJs understand what has happened to them and make meaning out of their life history. Their preference for Intuition helps them see all sides and leads to the understanding of paradox. Jim very elegantly expresses this.

While I am proud of, comfortable with, and thankful for seventy-four years, it is paradoxical, I guess, that for all my adult life I have felt stuck at the age of fourteen. Not a child anymore, but coming up well short of adulthood has its merits in being the age at which all the world is seen spread out like a smorgasbord to be devoured. It also has its demerits in being the age at which most everyone else has a head start. But both sides of the coin are valid. It is important to have one's own experiences and positions but not be too attached to them. I've learned that the essence of experience is what you make of it, and that you must learn to hold the two sides of things together gracefully. When there is a bad wind it is good for my sailing but bad for my fishing.

Late-life spiritual issues are interesting to these imaginative, honest people, but they are not often spoken of. There is a fear that words are incapable of communicating deep truths and worry that, in fact, words just might sound phony. Nevertheless, when asked, Jim did speak of meaning and of life and death in his own very individualistic manner, as one would expect.

I have no grand aha about all of this. I'm in a fog, but I know it is out there. One thing I have no doubt about, however: I'm part of a pool of spirit from which some little piece was drawn seventy-five years ago and put in this frame. I also think I'm working on letting go of my ego. Those stories about giving up self to find self and losing life to find life sound like nice Sunday morning talk. Well, it's not that nice, but I'm working on it. For me to forget my ego is to forget that anyone is looking, to not have to worry about who is coming up behind. The most important thing for me to do is be myself. I can do a lot of things, but others can do many of them better. The most important thing I can do is be whatever God— or whoever—put this raw material here to become.

Sylvia has similar feelings.

More and more I'm having to find my own way, and that's okay. I can't look to the church for spiritual nurturance. The preacher is a nice guy, but that can't do it. Preaching can't do it, either. Music helps keep me going.

Jim and Sylvia and others like them often had to find a very personal way toward the Divine—the way of the "God within."

ROSA AND CECILIA—ENTPs

Rosa, Age 74

Rosa, an ENTP, is a survivor of a major automobile accident. She is a very active, involved, and committed member of her community. This seventy-four-year-old wife, mother, and small-business owner has, over the years, been involved in most major civic organizations in her community, and has been president of several of them. In her sixties,

> *"You can't really guide people by telling them what to do, but you can support them in what they choose."*

with two grown children on their own, she completed a doctoral degree. "It was a lot of trouble for little benefit," she says nonchalantly, "but I did it." She has also taught at the university level and directed a major human potential and leadership program.

The telephone and doorbell interrupt our interview. "I don't like to turn the telephone off," she says, "for I might miss something." This active involvement is not new, but it is not as intense as it has been in the past.

After a major car accident when she was sixty-six, Rosa spent months unable to walk. Many of her friends and some of her doctors feared that she might not walk again. She does walk now, with only a slight limp, but the accident was a major turning point for her. "I had been slowing down before the accident," she said, "but it brought everything to a drastic halt. I was stopped in my tracks." She recalled a time some years before the accident.

> I was so exhausted. I was in a trap of activity and responsibility. I was raising children and working and serving on community boards. They all seemed important. Most of the time I was feeling that the world might crash if I didn't get something done the next minute. It took years to begin to get out of this. After my children left home I did have more time, and I was getting out of the trap before the accident, but the accident is what did it. Things are different now, though not entirely.

She explained that she had always been fighting against time, and she still does to some extent, but she has learned to relax. She can even "piddle around the house some," but not all the time. She can also "listen better to people without telling them what I think most of the time." Gradually, very gradually, she said she has learned that "you can't really guide people by telling them what to do, but you can support them in what they choose." She told me of a friend of hers who had many problems and made heavy demands on her time and patience. "I recently spent time with that woman," she said. "Earlier, I wouldn't have done that, for I would have seen it as a waste of my time. I'm being kinder to people, you might say."

Cecilia, Age 73

Cecilia is a seventy-three-year-old widow who is living with her daughter temporarily while she waits to get into a new retirement facility that is under construction. Her active, full life has been plagued by health problems, but her natural enthusiasm and optimism have served her well. Her MBTI type is ENTP.

Cecilia is grateful for the time with her daughter and son-in-law, but she is looking forward to moving to her new quarters with some positive, interesting people she knows who are also moving there. She says she thinks this will be "like going to college," and she is preparing to decorate

"from scratch." Cecilia is vivacious, optimistic, and respected by many as one who sees what is needed and responds in a direct way. She described herself as "imaginative in a very practical way."

> *My life recently has been controlled by my health problems. I have no use of one arm due to surgery for breast cancer years ago. I was forty-two when I had the surgery and thirty years ago breast surgery was in its infancy. They do better now, but I can't use that arm. Then this year I had to have my other shoulder replaced, and since that surgery I've really been unable to do things—even to care for myself. I used to be physical and I'm not anymore. I don't say, Why me? but I do say, Why? Yet I'm learning something. I'm learning to be patient, and I've never been patient. Now this is how it is and I must live with it.*

She talked about her philosophy of positive thinking. She warned that she must stay away from negative people. And she must stay away from critical, judging people as well, for they "affect her in a bad way."

> *You have to take the bad and find the good in it. When I had breast surgery it led me to establish a Reach for Recovery program. I convinced the medical profession and the American Cancer Society to support it—and I'll be happy to be remembered for that. Now I don't know what will come of my arm problem, but I feel on the edge of a whole new life. I believe something will come of this, although I don't know what it is. You know, you mustn't push too hard. I look at the health pages on the Internet now, and I'm also interested in studying spirituality. Who knows what will come. My legs and certainly my arms aren't too good now, but my head and mouth work well. I'm asking, What can I do with what I've got?*

Coming to Age as an ENTP

Rosa and Cecilia and others are learning not to push too hard, but they are independent, competent people, and as they age, this does not change. Yet they are always looking for opportunities. They also are developing the ability to listen better to themselves and to others. And when they see what is needed, they can commit to discovering all they can discover. Coming to age also brings an acceptance that they are being "looked after," as Cecilia commented.

After my cancer surgery, a young doctor told me I had a recurrence of cancer and put me on drugs and radiation. I was in bad shape. I staggered, saw spots in front of my eyes, and felt my blood running cold in my veins. I knew I was dying. I found another doctor, one who had a reputation for working with dying people. I wanted her to help me die. Late one night, after a lot of tests, she called and said she could find no signs of malignancy. She did say I had the lowest thyroid she could ever remember seeing. I'm not the kind who pays much attention to dreams or messages in the night, but during this period my dreams were so strong I had to get up in the night and write them down. I got five messages in one week. One was, "Be still and know that I am God." And the last one was, "Being led to the right doctor is a miracle in itself." I don't take this kind of thing at face value, but being led to the right doctor is a miracle. I've had bad things happen to me, but Someone is looking after me.

Looking back on her life, Cecilia sees a pattern. Her jobs, both paid and volunteer, have "just opened for her." Her Reach to Recovery work was possible after her cancer surgery because she had worked in hospitals and knew doctors and hospital systems. Enrolling in a class led to her involvement with a new and wonderful group of women and interesting work. "My life has been this way," she said. "Things open. I didn't make these things happen, but I'm not passive, either. Things *have* just happened, but I've always been looking, too."

Rosa also understands the importance of both receptivity and initiative. She has made peace with the fact that she is looking for something that she may never find, and is happy concentrating on the journey.

I'm looking for something. People are always talking about the journey. I know I'm on a journey. I'm heading toward something, but I don't know what. . . . I'm just a beginner here, but I have a lot of curiosity. I don't think I'm prepared for death. I guess I prepare by leading a full life. When I get discouraged I get up and get going. There is always something else to learn out there. I love to learn. There's so much I'll never touch.

Other ENTPs I spoke to talked about having in the coming to age period more gentleness and less pressure to accumulate experiences. One person said, "Now that I find myself freer from having to experience everything, I find that I am better able to experience what I really need to experience. I've come, at least sometimes, to know the difference between what is interesting and what is important." Rarely is this gift available to young ENTPs. Another spoke of the need for gentleness and reflection.

My edges are softer now. My early years were so full. I jumped from one interesting thing to another, but there was little time for reflection—or even for compassion, I'm now realizing. I didn't take time to think about or care for myself or anyone else. I now listen better. I accept more. I feel freer and not so driven to experience everything. Yet surprisingly I can experience a lot. I'm free to experience, but now I mostly want to make a difference in people's lives. That's new. It's exciting to make a difference in people's lives.

MARK, ELIZABETH, AND SOPHIE—ENTJs

Mark, Age 67

Mark is sixty-seven years old. His psychological type is ENTJ. He is married and associated with a major university in an administrative position, but previously he spent twenty-four years as a Roman Catholic priest. He entered seminary at seventeen and left the priesthood at forty-one. "In a funny way, I haven't left the priesthood," he said, "but it was very important to break with the institutional bureaucratic thing. I needed freedom to go my own way with theological questions, and there was the celibacy issue, too." He says that throughout his life, he has been tormented by religious questions. He used

> "It was very important to break with the institutional bureaucratic thing."

to worry about not being orthodox, but now he is much less concerned about that. He feels freer and enjoys his current connection to an institution, although he acknowledges that he may also need to look at that sometime. He spoke of that.

When you work for an institution you do have to be a good boy to that institution, but I'm now really happy to be doing fully what I care about—religion. I'm a searcher. When the president of my institution left for his vacation last year, he said, "Keep the faith, whatever that means to a searcher like you."

But Mark says his search is not primarily for growth, self-fulfillment, and personal meaning; he is an intellectual searcher.

> *I need to talk to others and know a lot about others' thought. I want to formulate and articulate intellectual understanding. I must say I find a certain selfishness about a too-personal spirituality. I want to make a difference in the world. If others want this, I want to work with them. But I don't want to waste my time. I want to know I make a difference, and I'm impatient with too much effort at finding something that is only personally satisfying. If people aren't interested in my approach, it's okay, but I think maybe they and I should have an amicable parting. Some people say my way is all "head stuff." It's not, and that attitude makes me angry. It's vital to me.*

His passion now is to formulate his positions on things and articulate them. He wants to be honest and faithful to his religious beliefs and to reach out to other "good, wise people who don't share my view. That's where my head is," he says.

> *Recently I wrote for publication an open letter to a Buddhist-Christian friend. I'm vitally interested in interfaith studies—Catholic, Protestant, Jewish, Buddhist, and Muslim. It took me two months to think through what I had to say, but now I have a position. I know where I stand, and it feels good. It was a tremendous feeling of being centered.*

Elizabeth, Age 79

Elizabeth, also an ENTJ, is a seventy-nine-year-old woman living in a retirement center with her husband of fifty years. A petite and youthful woman with a slight limp from an attack of polio suffered as a young woman, she sees herself as confident and even as "tough." Elizabeth and her husband are both admired as active, community-minded people who are still using their time and energy to "make things better."

> *Back when I was in my early thirties, polio was rampant. It took several children in our neighborhood, and finally it claimed our eight-month-old baby. Then I got it, too. My assistant minister*

came to our house and told me if I let it, this tragedy would ruin my life. I thought about it and decided I couldn't let it ruin my life. I owed things to the people who had provided scholarships for my education and to my husband and our remaining child, so I decided to assume a cheerful demeanor. I also decided to have another child, although I had been told I couldn't do that. At first we tried to adopt, but we got turned down. So I sat down and made a list of reasons to have a child and reasons not to. I decided to try to have the child. The doctor said I would lose the baby or have to abort, but I didn't. It was my small miracle. I'm tough.

I didn't sense a lot of regret in her life, but I asked her about the subject. She said she and her husband have had a **"I did feel guilty for a while, but I stopped it."** good life, though certainly not without struggle. Most of the struggles or concerns have been around finances and family. The loss of her baby was a devastating blow, of course, and their son had a difficult period growing up. "Maybe I should have done better—maybe I wasn't sensitive enough. I did feel guilty for a while, but I stopped it. I had tried hard and had been a better mother than most."

Elizabeth is currently very involved with her son, for his wife recently died and he is now caring alone for their young daughter. Grandparenting this child has become very important, and Elizabeth is committed to being there for the child.

Sophie, Age 65

Sixty-five-year-old Sophie is also an ENTJ. She explained that her home, which she built with and shares with her husband of forty-five years, as well as her yard with its perfectly manicured lawn, bountiful blooming azaleas, and weeping cherry tree, give her some of her greatest joy. She studied interior design for a short time after high school and has worked at a variety of jobs, but she has always primarily structured her life around her husband, children, and home. Sophie is very active. She works part time, writes, gardens, takes classes, and manages her family. She used one word over and over to describe herself and her life: "I'm lucky," she said, despite the losses in her life. "This period of life is about loss," she began. "At fifty, I was in a group that talked a lot about loss and I thought I understood, but I didn't. Then I started losing my friends to death." She explained that one of her three best friends had died suddenly of a stomach aneurysm. Shortly after, another developed lung cancer, and the third early Alzheimer's. "I learned about loss. This should have been further away for us, and I felt there but for the grace of God go I."

I haven't had any serious illnesses. I'm lucky, but it feels weird not to have anyone to run with and confide in. We [the four friends] used to have so much fun. I have my mother and daughter. And I have my husband. We do have fun, but he's not always interested in all I'm interested in. I'm not too worried about myself. I'm too busy, and besides, it's better that way. I try not to worry about us. My life is overflowing.

"I say look for doors and push them. Don't ever give up."

Sophie has a part-time job in a shop that she and her husband own, and she writes, knits, and loves television. She loves to garden. "I'm a dirt gardener," she says. "I come home from the shop and rush into the yard to mow and work for a couple of hours." She is also looking forward with great enthusiasm to visiting her first grandson.

I asked Sophie about the struggles and limitations she had experienced in her life.

My strict orthodox Jewish upbringing limited me. It limited my friends. I was told never to date a Gentile, although I did once [she laughed]. I also remember and have written about being called "Jew baby" by my classmates. And I've been held back by being female. You know, when I was young, schools had Jewish quotas, and even the boys had trouble getting into law school and medical school. We weren't, as Jewish girls, to even think of taking one of those spots. And now it's ageism, but I've learned to fight. I say look for doors and push them. Don't ever give up. Don't sit down.

Coming to Age as an ENTJ

Enthusiasm, optimism, and lack of inclination to concentrate on past tragedies mark these ENTJs creatively coming to age. They have learned that joy and pain are often close kin—Mark with the loss of one kind of priesthood and the finding of another, Elizabeth with the loss of her baby and with the current relationship to her grandchild, and Sophie with her growing up with prejudice and limitation and her current openness and gratitude for all that life can bring.

Mark has learned to find and express his own position.

I've been holding things in for years. Now I'm able to articulate what I really think if I have time to think it through. I used to be hesitant and tactful because I didn't want to stir up conflict and also because I have the intellectual's paralysis—seeing all sides of everything. Now, when I have time to get my head around it, I can find the position that is mine.

Elizabeth speaks matter-of-factly and very pragmatically about the end of her life.

I'm not afraid of dying, although I should like to do it fast and painlessly and leave no remains to worry with. We, at our age, are all going downhill and we're going to die. But I don't think much about it. Just do as much good as you can and have a good time.

Sophie also wants to cause little trouble for others and also thinks very pragmatically.

I have a book about the Hemlock Society, but I haven't read it. The Jewish religion frowns on suicide and thinks life support is up to the family. My husband and I have nursing home insurance, and I have a living will. All I know to do is take charge as much as you can. There's not a lot you can do, and things keep changing. I do believe in God. How else would those azaleas be blooming like they are?

CONCLUSION

So, in general, how are these people different in the coming to age period than they were in their earlier lives? What joys are they experiencing that were reserved for their later years? I suggest that they can claim a sense of connectedness and relatedness that was rarely available to them when they were young. They are more connected with and related to themselves because they accept themselves with fewer demands and more tenderness. They are able to make decisions with their hearts as well as their heads. They are more connected to others, and may find delight in teaching and mentoring them. They are more able to connect the global with the immediate and the abstract with the personal. They feel less isolated and sometimes feel connected to Something outside themselves as well, often through the arts, through nature, or through the mystic's "God within." They can lay down their armor—at least on good days—and other people can feel more accepted and respected in their presence.

They are becoming more accepting of themselves and their way of being in the world. One man, when asked what change in himself pleased him the most, answered, "I have come to love myself." With more self-acceptance, these Intuitive Thinking people are able to be less defended and more vulnerable. They can state their positions with less need to impose them on others. Their tenderness as they are coming to age stems, at least in part, from a desire to be of service, and particularly to be of service in the Intuitive Thinking way of changing structures, communicating, and teaching. They've learned to connect knowledge and action, the global and the personal.

CHAPTER 7

JOY AND DEVOTION

Guilt and the threat of exclusion from the
community serve as powerful deterrents to
the development of the individual.

—James Hollis

SF Joy and devotion are unexpected joys of the later years for these practical, realistic, grounded people who value community approval and action—characteristics associated with preferences for Sensing and Feeling. As these people age, they learn to hold the tension between their needs for stability and clarity and for new stimulation and risk taking. They come closer to defining their own personal vision—a definition that does not rely on others —and they bring sustained commitment to that vision. They are better able to balance reflective time with action and to discern when they should intervene and when they should not. They find a relationship between play and work. For the person who prefers Sensing and Feeling, creatively coming to age means learning to transform heavy obligation into devotion and frivolous fun into joy.

$\mathcal{T}$he well-developed Sensing Feeling types (ISFJ, ESFJ, ISFP, ESFP) have been described as practical, realistic, solid, helping, and present oriented. They are people who perceive what is presented to them and act on it. They are grounded people who care greatly about providing a good life for themselves and others. They trust experience, both their own and that of others, as their teacher. Whether they are fun-loving, outgoing ESFPs, socially sensitive ESFJs, quiet, gentle ISFPs, or cautious, caring ISFJs, they all bring a sense of receptivity, attentiveness, and humility to life. They desire to serve their communities, and they love and need community—perhaps, at times, too much.

As children, they are generally realistic, active, and pleasant. Whether in the more playful way of the SFPs or the more serious "little adult" way of the SFJs, they enjoy their involvement with others, particularly if they can serve and be appreciated. They are usually in touch with, and quite influenced by, what is happening around them.

At midlife, the Sensing Feeling people are often nudged by life toward further growth. Rather than simply a desire for personal growth, it is events that interrupt their life structure, such as a geographic move or a relationship or job change, that frequently call their attention to a need for midlife adjustment. Or sometimes it is a book, or a workshop, or a friend's experience that leads the Sensing Feeling people, particularly the SFJs, to wonder if they are missing something, or if they are not prepared for a change that they "should be making." Sometimes excessive, meaningless activity can awaken the active SFPs with questions of meaning and nudge the diligent, prone-to-burnout SFJs into midlife transition. As midlife questions arise, Sensing Feeling people can feel overwhelmed and immobilized, or they can move too quickly in order to escape the painful experience of being stuck. They may feel frightened and immobilized as they find themselves being led toward territory that seems overly risky, too esoteric, unsafe, or just plain "weird." Or they may find themselves acting too quickly in order to avoid the discomfort of not being able to act. The discomfort with ambiguity and lack of clarity experienced by these Sensing Feeling people is often accompanied by a fear of disconnection from community that midlife growth—or any growth for that matter—can produce. The pull toward a more authentic personal identity and a broader vision may be seen by them as detrimental to the community they so desire.

Like many others, they struggle with issues of defining themselves and staying related to others, but it seems the Sensing Feeling people's primary need is to belong to a community they can serve and be appreciated by, rather than one that "respects" them or one that "simply helps them grow." In fact, many Sensing Feeling type people are suspicious of too much emphasis on personal growth. Rather, their emphasis is often toward "good works." As one ISFP man said, "I can tell you I don't remember, or care, what my mother said to me when I was ten, but I care a great deal about what is happening to abused children in this community."

As these grounded, realistic givers of care broaden their vision and discover their own authentic identity apart from community definition, as they commit to their own true calling, they may find that they can serve tirelessly with spontaneous joy and committed devotion. They may find that they are not as likely to be held back by such things as denial, fear, guilt, anxiety, blame, and dependence. And they may be delighted to find that they can age creatively, avoiding an old age marked by sour compulsion, rigidity, or a flighty inability to commit.

As they age creatively and claim their own authentic identity and personal vision, these people feel more confident with less need to be continually reassured

Fear does not block as often, and courage seems to have arrived unbidden.

and limited by others' opinions. They find they require from others only what the others have to give, and that they themselves need not feel guilty when they give only what they can give. They may find that a newer and deeper community arises, and that it does not depend on conformity. And almost without their knowing it, anxiety often subsides. As one person said, "It stops tearing at my throat." Fear does not block as often, and courage seems to have arrived unbidden. And these realistic, present-oriented people may be surprised and delighted to discover spontaneity and lightness (particularly the SFJs) as well as commitment (particularly the SFPs). They may discover *both* joy and devotion at the same time, a gift rarely available to the Sensing Feeling people when they are young.

Joyful devotion is about fidelity and commitment characterized not by duty or obligation, but by delight. It is commitment voluntarily chosen and blissfully embraced. Joy and devotion come to the Sensing Feeling people when they realize that they have a unique and special vision to which they can commit out of a sense of their own identity and their own call. Joyful devotion comes when they are able to make their unique vision manifest without a sense of weariness, heaviness, or confinement. It is present when, as one person put it, "we dream the possible dream, and not only dream it, but do it."

Joy and devotion are marked by commitment, hope, optimism, freshness, and spontaneity. They are unblemished by blaming, fear, and anxiety. Joyful devotion comes to Sensing Feeling people when they can act with courage and with sustained commitment without fear of failure or of disapproval. It comes when the caregivers include themselves in the circle of care.

Joy and devotion allow Sensing Feeling people to serve the collective with true confidence and true humility, knowing that they are doing what is theirs to do and that this is only a part of the whole. Others experience them as committed, approachable, and at ease with themselves and often feel peaceful and safe in their presence.

Now meet a few of these creatively aging people. Listen closely and you will know what they have to teach us about joy and devotion, and about how life has both changed them and left them the same.

LUCRETIA, PAT, AND CHRISTINE—ISFJs

Lucretia, Age 70

Lucretia is a community-minded, active woman of seventy years who is an ISFJ. She lives happily in her beloved hometown. Lucretia grew up in a small, friendly community as an only child and, after a short time away to attend college, she returned home to teach. She now lives alone and feels safe and connected. "Maybe I'm narrow or naive from staying close to home, but I'm glad, too. I love this community and all the people in it," she began. Her continuing love for her community is expressed through her active role of service in public life. She has organized several class reunions and is currently working on a program to change legal restrictions so that older women can rent out rooms in their homes more freely and therefore have the financial resources to continue to live in their homes. She loves the smallness and caring of her community. She said she doesn't feel old,

> "The biggest change is about not having to impress so much."

although she does find some aches and pains to be inconvenient and she fears that "if she sits down she'll never get up." Sitting down does not seem to be her problem. She showed me her calendar. Every daily block on it is filled with appointments, and the appointments are color coded. "Maybe I'm too busy," she said, "but I like to be active."

> I don't relax very well, and that was true when I was young. My high school yearbook said I was a worrier, and I still am. I'm structured and organized, and I like to know what's going on. I also have a little money now, and I enjoy it. I joined a golf club and buy season tickets to the opera. I enjoy my independence. I do miss some people who are gone, but I know I can't bring them back. And although I would like to have someone with me, I enjoy my independence. I do what I want and I'm not lonely. The biggest change is about not having to impress so much. The difference between my fifth and fortieth class reunions was astonishing. I still want to be at the top, but it's not as important. I am what I am and I've done my thing.

The need to impress, to "do the right thing," and the need not to hurt others can lead ISFJs away from themselves. But age and maturity—and the ISFJ backbone of steel that is not far beneath the surface—often come to the rescue.

Pat, Age 62

Pat, who is sixty-two years old, is living happily in a rented room in the home of a friend after the breakup of her thirty-seven-year marriage. Her psychological type is ISFJ. Pat is planning to retire soon from her longtime career as a nurse.

> I don't know where I'm going, but it will be somewhat like the past. I've been a nurse and nurturer for more than forty years, but now the stress is too high in nursing. The profession is driven by money, not by service, and I don't think I should have to push so hard at this time in my life. I'll have to do something to make some money, and it will be something similar to things I've already done. I'll find a way to serve—maybe in a retirement center or a bookstore, or maybe working with Meals on Wheels. It will probably have something to do with the elderly.

Pat, like other ISFJs I interviewed, was perplexed when I asked about what has held her back. I wanted to know if things in her life and/or in herself had kept her from becoming the kind of person she wanted to be and doing what she wished to do. She had more interest in how she *acted* when she recognized things that held her back than in speculating about intrapsychic or environmental dynamics that could block her. After some contemplation, Pat decided that her husband's opposition to her advanced education and her wish not to offend him may have held her back—but only for a little while.

> *"Tell younger people not to wait as long as I did to pay attention to themselves."*

> *Before my mid-forties, I really did look upon myself as a vessel for everyone else. I thought that was my role and that my family, my friends, and my church liked me that way. I guess that kept me from moving sooner. But when you know something, the question is, What are you going to do about it? Tell younger people not to wait as long as I did to pay attention to themselves. And tell them when they are in a place they can't accept, the question is, Where do I go from here?*

I asked Pat how she would like to be remembered.

> *Earlier I would have wanted to be remembered as a good, fair mother who did well in her marriage and job. Now I want to be remembered as being the best I could be in the situations I've found myself in. I want to be remembered as one who didn't back away from difficult situations, as someone to be counted on, and as someone true to my word. I'm not wishy-washy.*

Christine, Age 84

Christine is an eighty-four-year-old ISFJ who is widely known as a wise helper and a loving person. And though primarily confined to her home by disabling arthritis, she serves with joy as well as devotion. She has developed good personal boundaries. She does not let people "play her," and she agreed to meet with me—after checking me out—because, she says, she sees this book project as "worthwhile."

She welcomed me warmly, although we had not previously met, and ushered me to a chair facing her big chair, which sat in front of her wide front window. She offered a table and a legal pad to make me comfortable, and she settled into her chair, which allowed her to view everything that was going on outside as well as inside the house.

Her room was filled with photographs of her "children." Christine has never married and has no biological children or living close blood relatives, but her home is filled with pictures of her adopted sons and daughters—most of whom are distant relatives or members of her church. One immediately notices that her children represent many races. "Don't call me Black," she instructs me. "You don't call people a color. And don't call me African American, either. I don't know anything about Africa. I'm American and my family is White, Indian, and Negro." She then laughs at herself for scolding me, but she is quite serious.

> *"When I've done what I can, I say, 'I've done all I can do. Let's don't talk anymore.' I must not waste my time."*

> We're all God's children. No one knows what to say, but that Black and African American stuff is from the sixties and seventies. I don't need that. I know who I am. I'm glad I know who I am. I'm glad I was born into the family I was born into. I know my parents, my grandparents, my aunts and uncles. I don't have to ask who I'm related to. Today many people don't know who they're related to, but I do. I've got a little bit of everything. Not everything has been good, but that's how you grow. You have to go through the rough and the good. But we have so many beautiful things. We don't have to concentrate on the ugly.

Recognizing her physical pain and inability to move easily, and realizing that her telephone had rung three times during our conversation from people just wanting to check in, I ask if this activity exhausts her. "No," she tells me emphatically. "It makes me happy." But she goes on. "People will, however, play you, so I'm glad for my business sense. When I've done what I can, I say, 'I've done all I can do. Let's don't talk anymore.' I must not waste my time."

Christine also talks about being positive. "People say they feel restful with me. I tell them to leave the negative outside. It isn't that negative things don't exist, but I don't concentrate on them." And she talked about what she wanted to say to the next generation.

> I want people to understand we have a lot to be thankful for, and I want them to put thankfulness into action. Some of the young people today—not all of them—think someone owes them. No one owes

*them anything. I get upset when I hear that a thirteen-year-old shot
a ten-year-old child and his mother says, "He's a good boy." It's not
a good boy who shoots his neighbor. And it's the senior generation's
fault. No one taught him that life is precious, that you can't just do
what you want to do, but you must do the right thing.*

Christine's joy of life is matched by her enthusiasm about death.
"It's the greatest thing," she says.

*I don't know why people don't want to talk about death. I don't
mean be morbid about it, but talk about it. I'm looking for the glorious life He has prepared for me. I'll know when my time comes
and I'll wake up someplace else and give thanks. Death is beautiful,
but I'm not in a hurry. I want to stay here. I'm doing God's will
and I would like to live a little longer so I can be helpful.*

Coming to Age as an ISFJ

The lack of "wishy-washy" characteristics, the backbone, the task orientation and work ethic that are lifetime companions of ISFJs do not
vanish in later life. In fact, one rarely gets "off the hook" with these people. One ISFJ said this to me:

*When someone says to me, "I want to, but I can't," I think, "You
just don't want to enough." Nevertheless, as I get older, I sometimes
wonder if maybe they really can't. I also don't feel as often that I
have to do everything for them, and I feel less annoyed with their
inability—at least as long as they don't whine.*

This softening of judgment and sharing of responsibility allows the
successfully aging ISFJ to move toward commitment that is marked by
joy and devotion, not simply by duty. Responsibility and determination
are still valued, but they can feel less burdensome. Blame, guilt, and
anxiety lessen and are often tempered by spontaneity, relaxation, humor,
optimism, and a grateful heart—often a heart that is grateful that it can
still do what others feel they cannot.

Lucretia, Pat, and Christine live carefully planned lives. Planning is a
way of being more certain "not to be dependent," which can be a greater
fear than loneliness or death. Over and over, these introspective, grounded
people, with their rich inner lives, said that although they miss people who
are no longer available, they are not lonely. They love independence and

psychological space as they age. They are most relaxed and joyful when they can move freely and without too many obligations in a safe, secure environment. Relationships that are marked by dependability and loyalty are most valued.

Like many other ISFJs, Lucretia, Pat, and Christine talk also of how they have come to value optimism. Statements such as "I'm an encourager" and "I leave the negative outside" are common. And these people often speak of the need to "look at the good side of people." An eighty-seven-year-old retired male teacher told me, "I admire people who have a positive outlook, people who are good-natured and don't go around criticizing folks all the time."

These and other ISFJs perceive primarily through their senses and often attach a very personal interpretation to what they perceive. If they speak about spiritual experience, the meaning of life, and other ultimate concerns, it is from their own experiences. Responses can range from humanistic and skeptical responses about the possibility of any life beyond the one experienced by the senses to responses that resemble what I call grounded mysticism. Even those who seem to be in personal touch with a Power beyond themselves require reassurance and often ground their conversation with at least some of the language of religious tradition. Even mystical experience is usually expressed in traditional language of "doing God's will."

> *I wish I could believe like some of my friends, but I really believe heaven and hell are here on Earth. I can't understand this stuff about the body dying and the soul going somewhere else. How would all the souls go up there? It's not clear. I wish it were.*

Another ISFJ spoke of her mystical leanings.

> *You have to go to that place. It's more than going to church. I always went to church. . . . [Now] I meditate, pray, and just talk to God, like a friend. . . . I feel the Presence. Only last week I had been feeling sad and it was twilight time. I just sat outside on my steps. It was getting dark and the automatic lights were coming on. Then my nostrils were filled with the wonderful fragrance of honeysuckle. I said, Thank-you. I know you're here. Thank-you.*

Community with others is an important part of the ISFJ personality, even in matters of spirituality. "Church is my family," Christine told me. It was that simple.

JO AND DAWN—ESFJs

Jo, Age 69

Optimism, joy, love of life, and humor mark the life of Jo, an ESFJ, who is planning for her later life by training herself to be alone. Jo is one of seven sisters who grew up in the south of Scotland. She is now separated from her husband and at sixty-nine is full of enthusiasm and fun. She spoke with candor and humor, and in a self-effacing way, about the process of aging.

> *My life is just ordinary stuff. Anyone could say what I have to say. But I'll tell you, I detest the idea of aging. There is so much beauty and so little time. I don't think of myself as old—that would be comical—but I have noticed my body doesn't obey me in ways it used to. With me there have been little sudden things, like a knee that doesn't work well or shoulder pain, and I think parts of me are falling apart. I'm a physical person, and I don't go on tirades against the body problems, but sometimes I feel like screaming a silent scream. Or sometimes I forget something and I think, "Oh, my God, how awful. I forgot that." I'm the way I always was, and I can't say this aging has taught me anything except that I need to exercise more and keep up my body tone.*

She spoke of practical things, such as planning for her later years and working on learning to be alone. She finds comfort in the routine and stresses the importance of having fun.

> *I need a lot of people around me but I'm training myself to be alone and not be lonely. It helps to have an "alone hobby." I've started quilting, and I can sit with the radio or listen to classical music and quilt happily by myself. I like to work and I like routine. That may sound funny, but routine sets parameters and it con-tributes to a function. I like to be busy—I've never been good at having nothing to do. I keep my calendar full, but I'm not a worka-holic. I love movies and golf. I play golf at least four times a week. When I retire I'll play more.*

Jo feels it's important not to take life too seriously.

> *I find things funny and that takes me, through the day. People take themselves so seriously that you have to laugh. They talk and talk*

and worry and worry. Maybe I'm just easily amused, but there is so much funny activity to observe. I had a wonderful childhood and parents, and I really wouldn't change much about my life. I'm lucky, and I certainly don't worry about what my mother said to me when I was eight years old. I do recognize my silliness sometimes. Growing up, I was one of the silliest girls in the south of Scotland. I was always with dogs and cats and hens. I went to a college for silly people. And I could say "how appalling," but I say, "Why not?" Childhood goes so fast, and it's lovely to look back on silliness. Why not? I hope I can give folks a few laughs. Humor and the physical feeling of laughter—not that tedious nervous giggling after every sentence and not laughter at "jokes," but real laughter—makes me feel filled with joy. I feel released.

Jo also has some things to say to those coming behind her.

Tell young people that your judgment is better in your fifties and sixties because you have more experience and are "saner." Tell young women that life is not over in the fifties and sixties. In fact, it's more carefree after menopause. It's a good time for sex. The fifties and sixties are fun.

Dawn, Age 66

Dawn is sixty-six years old, and her psychological type is ESFJ. She has been married for forty years. She told me she still often plays bridge with and entertains old

> "What I've learned is that we really can't change people."

friends and neighbors from previous neighborhoods, and she values these friendships. "I've been playing bridge with some of these people for twenty-two years. I know them and their families, and I surely wouldn't want to lose touch with them." Golf, bridge, travel, and especially her family and other relationships are all part of her zest for living.

I once heard a quote that I like a lot. It was something like, "We do not stop playing because we grow older. We grow older because we stop playing." I took up golf at fifty because my boys said I was over the hill, and I set out to prove I still had it. I can do what I put my mind to. And that's a good thing, because at sixty I lost the wonderful job I had had for twenty-three years when my company closed *its doors. I had been administrative assistant to the president of that company and had supervised a staff of secretaries. I loved that company and that work. We were like a family.*

I asked Dawn how she handled challenges and setbacks.

Life isn't easy. I wish someone had told me that when I was younger so I could have prepared better for it. But I just keep on one day at a time. I pray a lot and I do a lot of work. It's not pray or work, it's both. I'm really upset now because of a couple of family situations. I'm the primary person responsible for an aunt with dementia. I love her and I love to help her, but it is hard, for she may have to move and she doesn't have enough money to live in the kind of place she will want to live in. She will be sad, but I'm still trying to find the right place for her that she can afford. Also, one of our sons has just gotten a divorce and there are children. I don't want to accept this. When my husband and I learned about the divorce possibility, we went to a counselor for help. The counselor helped us understand that there was really nothing we could do to save the marriage. We couldn't get them back together and we couldn't get them to communicate. That was hard! I hate conflict and sadness, and I usually try to avoid it.

Dawn is in the process of writing her first book. To date she has taken a class to learn more about writing and has done a number of interviews and secured a publisher for her book in process.

It's going to be a happy book, full of memories and anecdotes that I'm getting through interviews. It'll have stories about families that our business worked with over the years and even some recipes for dishes served in our restaurant. And I guess it'll have a little sadness—there was sadness when we had to close the business. It'll have a little sadness, but not too much.

Dawn feels that, for her, coming to age has meant learning about limitations in relationships and accepting them.

What I've learned is that we really can't change people. I've been married for forty years. We have a good marriage, but my husband and I are almost opposites. A wise woman once told me, "You're not going to change him." And I don't try. If I want to do something,

I can do it alone or with friends, and he doesn't have to do everything with me. I don't like to cry, and I don't like to accept unhappy things like divorce and dementia. I don't like to rock the boat, but I do persevere. You can say, I guess, that I have a strong constitution. When things go wrong you just have to go on.

Coming to Age as an ESFJ

Jo and Dawn and others like these active, zestful, enthusiastic people can barely think of themselves as not being in control of their lives or able to care for themselves. They articulate some concerns and worries, but they do not focus on regrets. They focus on the positive. Jo says she doesn't regret much—not even her failed marriages.

I'm amicably separated now. Marriage is confining, and I like to do my own thing. Boredom is my nemesis. I'm now content, tranquil, and satisfied. I don't know what happy is, but I'm comfortable and I like comfort. I have a low threshold for pain. I've been a terrible coward about pain my whole life and I have to live with this. I cope by staying active, and I talk to my sisters about things that bother me. We talk about painful and fearful things. We take the sutures out and look, but we don't think and talk things to death. That would be appalling, for we get together to have some fun. But we do try to stare down the pain.

Jo and Dawn and other successfully aging ESFJs work, and they work for the love of their work, not because something is required of them. They do what they have to do without feeling overburdened and without appearing overbearing to others or making others feel obligated. They include themselves in their circle of care, and they have learned not to expect to meet approval and affirmation on every front. Dawn talked about caregiving at its best, caregiving that does not deplete nor obligate, but that is done for the love of doing.

I like to be busy. I have people over a lot and I do a lot for them. I serve shrimp often and I peel every shrimp. People say, why do you go to all that trouble? You do so much and make work for yourself. I do make work, but our friends enjoy those shrimp and I get enjoyment from that. My husband loves pickles and peach cobbler, so I make those things. I like him to enjoy it. He will ask me why I read three stories for my grandchildren when I only promised to read one. I love my grandchildren, and they want me to read a lot to them. I do it because it makes them happy and it makes me happy, too—happy inside.

Jo and Dawn and other ESFJs spend little time "unpacking" the meaning of life. They often think of leaving life as they think of living life. Jo spoke simply, plainly, and honestly from her own experience.

I think of death as dreamless sleep, the same as before we're born. I was not, now I am, and one day I won't be. I don't mind the idea of perpetual oblivion. Getting to that is the problem, since I'm a coward and afraid of pain. And I don't really feel connected to anything other than my everyday experience. I feel harmony, beauty, and rhythm in nature. I feel absorbed in it sometimes, but I don't think of myself as a spiritual person. See, I don't want to unravel it. It just is, and I'm willing to dwell in it the best way possible.

And for Dawn, who enjoys peeling shrimp for her friends and cooking cobbler for her husband, perhaps death may allow for one last gift.

My husband and I have decided to give our bodies to science. That makes me feel good, too. Life is good, and if my body can help someone else, fine. The ground has too many people, anyway.

KATHLEEN AND ANNE—ISFPs

Kathleen, Age 84
The gentle, kind, and adventurous Kathleen is an ISFP. At eighty-four, she is one of three people over eighty whom I interviewed. She is beloved by young people and is frequently selected by them as a role model. Her comments about aging, death, and dying carry a matter-of-fact acceptance.

Kathleen lives in the home she and her late husband built over forty years ago. She has been widowed for more than three decades, and has lived all of that time alone in this house in a small, sleepy southern town where "we look after each other" and "don't worry much about break-ins." She has a married daughter living in the same town, and recently her unmarried son moved back into the home with her. Earlier in her life she was a public school teacher and an active community citizen. She has traveled extensively, as her wide interests and her lack of attachments have allowed her to do. She now travels little and is

> *"As you age you realize there are things you can't do anything about, and anyway, things work out."*

very concerned about her failing hearing. Although she occasionally may forget a name or a date, her memory is quite sharp. She began to tell me her experience of the process of aging.

> *One day I looked in the mirror and I was old, with sagging skin and such. Time moves so fast. I can remember when the after-noons—particularly in the summer—were so long. You would wait and wait for husbands to come home and for eating supper. Time flies now. I like it when people come to see me, for a lot of my friends are gone, and even those of us who are left can't correspond as well as we did. Some people can't see to read what you've written them, and I don't go out as much as I did. I do, however, go to small groups, although I don't hear a lot of what is going on. People don't speak as clearly as they once did. [She laughs.]*
>
> *Sometimes younger people try to help too much and I feel hur-ried. We have to get used to slowing down. Sometimes even going from one room to another is a real challenge—it can be a long way from the living room to the bedroom. It didn't used to matter where I hung my hat, but now I like things to stay the same. It's hard to change bedrooms. It is hard not to worry, too, but it used to be harder. As you age you realize there are things you can't do any-thing about, and anyway, things work out.*

Kathleen has paid attention to her life, and she had a few things to say to those who are a bit younger. She had thought her advice through, and she intended to be helpful. "Tell the younger ones to get a hobby, take care of their physical body, and make some new younger friends. Everyone needs to get a hobby or an interest or something you won't get tired of," she said. She has made many attempts at hobbies, including a bricklaying class that was going to help her build a little brick wall in her yard. The wall didn't get built and the bricklaying interest didn't last, but the sense of exploration did. She tried china painting, and she rejoices that some of her classmates loved it for years, but "I couldn't get the little roses right." She instead settled into "learning everything I could about the fourteenth century." Why the fourteenth century? "The fourteenth century was interesting," was her simple explanation. "I might still decide to learn everything I can about some important person. I've been thinking about that. I can still do that. I can go down to the library and check out some books."

Not only does she see the importance of staying mentally alert, but she sees a need to stay physically active also. "It is good as you age to do a little something for your physical body," she said. "I used to walk a lot, but I turned my ankle. It's hard to get back to exercise when you stop. Better not to stop, but you can get back little by little."

"And also people need to make some new friends as well as keep their old ones, if they can." She told me about one of her friends whose interest was getting married. "She got married three times," Kathleen reported, "but that wasn't my hobby. Yet you do need friends. It's awful to be isolated, but you need freedom, too. I don't want someone underfoot all the time."

Kathleen once wanted to be a writer. "I didn't really want to write. I just wanted to be a writer," she laughed, with a sense of humor and of the acceptance that can come with seeing and loving one's limitations.

Anne, Age 68

Anne is sixty-eight years old and retired. Her psychological type is ISFP. She talked about her sense of service and her joyful commitment to what she believes in.

Anne swims every day, is active in her church, photographs her many travels, and regularly takes into her home children who need care. I noticed nestled among her things a series of puppets that she uses in her storytelling to the children. Divorced from an alcoholic and abusive spouse, she has three grown sons and several grandchildren. At the time of my visit, she was looking forward to a summer trip with

> "I don't like to talk about myself, and I don't like to talk about my problems. I prefer to do something."

one of her grandchildren. Her family life has presented her with many challenges and considerable pain, and she points out that perhaps this is why she is so willing to help children in need. She does not appear to have any sense of martyrdom about her life; rather, she exhibits a sense of devotion and commitment. Her voice is soft and unassuming as she relates her experiences with the children she welcomes into her home.

I'm action oriented. I don't like to talk about myself, and I don't like to talk about my problems. I prefer to do something. I tutor and mentor children who need academic help. I keep runaways and children waiting to get into residential homes. Some of the children I've had can't go home because their parents don't want them. Some of them are actually living in cars with their boyfriends. Usually I give them my bed and sleep on the couch. Being on the couch allows me to see them if they try to get out the door. Most of the children I keep are really emergencies, and if I don't take them in they have to go to juvenile detention homes. Usually they don't stay very long, but I kept one young girl for five weeks.

I told her I admire her commitment, but this didn't feel like the correct word to describe what she does. Devotion would have been a better choice. And it is devotion with a strong dose of realism.

I don't look at it that way. I look at it as a way to help children. I don't think anything about it. Sometimes it just gives them a cooling down time, but sometimes they do take advantage of me. I had two run. One girl said she wanted to go for a walk and I let her take my watch—the one my father gave me when I went away to school. She didn't come back. Another came to me through social services because she was spending nights in her boyfriend's car. She was a case. She wanted me to chauffeur her around to her boyfriend and she turned down every job that came along. I had to get tough with her. But the girl who stayed five weeks got straightened out. She wrote to me for a year.

Coming to Age as an ISFP

The gentle, caring Anne, like many other ISFPs consciously coming to age, has come to recognize the danger of naiveté, or the tendency to unconsciously accept what life presents. "I grew up in a home where we all sat down for supper together each night and we thought most people were basically nice," says Anne. "I really thought other people sat down to dinner together each night and were basically nice. They don't, and they aren't."

These ISFPs have become aware of aging not by personal soul searching, but by noticing their aging bodies and their experiences. Anne laughingly told me that the day she realized she was aging was a nice warm day in early summer when she put on her bathing suit for the first time since the summer before and "had a look in the mirror."

Kathleen and Anne and other ISFPs need to find something they won't get tired of and that they can commit to with devotion and joy. These things are almost always close at hand—as close as a library, a friend, or a needy child. Life is lived in the everyday; it is about acceptance, even of decline and the end of physical life. "I'm not afraid of dying," says Kathleen.

> I'll just be lying over there in a grave and I'll enjoy being alone someplace else. What's the choice? When you can't live, you die. There may be a Great Plan. I think there must be. I know there is a rhythm, a time to live and a time to die. Afterward someone else must come along. It would be awful to have all the people who ever lived living at one time. The planet couldn't take it. I think heaven is different for each person. No one knows what it is like, and we're never going to get there in this life, but striving toward it is fun. I used to think a lot about these kinds of things, but I don't anymore. No use.

She speaks with acceptance, detachment, compassion, and humor.

Acceptance of "whatever will be" is real, but creatively aging ISFPs also realize the importance of paying attention and learning from what is happening to them. They learn not to accept things too easily and to take their experiences more seriously. As one woman said, "I used to say, 'I don't make mountains out of molehills.' I still don't, but now I also don't make molehills out of mountains."

DAVID AND JON—ESFPs

David, Age 72

David is a retired Protestant minister, seventy-two years old, and an ESFP. He lives with his wife and works part time as a spiritual director and occasional liturgist. Many people seek him out, and he is often described as "caring" and "outgoing." He sees himself as having a lot of "feminine energy" and in some ways being more comfortable in the company of women than in the company of men.

"There are some things that I never plan to make peace with. One of these is racism, and another is exclusivity."

David's realistic, down-to-earth nature is characterized by an expression he likes to use: "Taking care of the dirt." This expression stems from a story about a family funeral.

The funeral was completed, the casket was in the ground, and the people directing the funeral were obviously waiting for us to leave the gravesite before they tossed the dirt on the lowered casket. I didn't want to leave, so I picked up the shovel and tossed the first shovel of dirt. The other people then left to go to the gathering that was being held after the service, but I hung back and filled that grave with dirt. I've been told that someone at the reception asked where I was, and a friend said, "He's taking care of the dirt." That's just what I was doing.

David talked about how he is different in his seventies from the way he was in his forties and fifties.

My flashpoint is higher. I tend to back off some when it really doesn't matter too much, rather than passionately taking a stand as I once did. Yet there are some things that I never plan to make peace with. One of these is racism, and another is exclusivity. I now want to be more contemplative and really want to not be attached to anything but God. My image of my work has shifted from preaching and teaching to helping people bring forth out of their own lives. I now think the body is as important as the spirit and the mind. That's a change for me. I sometimes think my dietitian is my spiritual director. Of course, she doesn't know she is.

While David is becoming more committed, more reflective, and less volatile, he continues to live life with the ESFP liveliness, grace, and sense of humor.

Jon, Age 72

Jon, also an ESFP, is a retired man of seventy-two who has spent most of his life in a nonfitting career and has recently become "unlocked" from it by retirement. His "life statement," he told me, might be something like, "What we keep, we lose. Only what we give away remains our own." He talked about learning this and other things.

"What we keep, we lose. Only what we give away remains our own."

My marriage and parenthood made me grow up. I have a lot of child in me, and I did once think I was immortal. Why, I didn't even look when I crossed the street until I had responsibilities. Family has made me face facts, and that might make marriage sound stifling, but it doesn't have to be. In our early marriage, my wife and I never fought. Now, if no one in a marriage is ever arguing, it means someone is being subservient. That's how it was early in my marriage, but then my wife went to assertiveness training. This nice, sweet southern girl went to assertiveness training and things became more alive, more confrontational. It was really unsettling, and it took a lot to stabilize the marriage. We are really both better for this, though.

Jon says that he and his wife do communicate well, and that humor serves them well, too. He believes that humor and variety serve well as people age. He elaborated:

People without humor bore me. Remember old Boxer in Animal Farm? *He just went up one row and down another and never questioned. I know a brilliant man—a religious man—who does this. He doesn't seem able to enjoy life. Everything is so serious for him. He's on "a course."*

For Jon there is really a time to laugh at things and, as he said, "to laugh at oneself also." Jon spends a lot of time laughing and relatively little time on regrets, but he does wish he had paid more attention to his finances, especially to retirement planning. He also wishes he had been more aware of the consequences of some relationships; but finally he tells me he finds "life mistakes" not something to be dwelt on but just "grist for the mill." As life moves on, he is learning to accept it, and there is peace and a lack of struggle with that.

Coming to Age as an ESFP

To Jon and David and many other creatively aging ESFPs, the meaning of their later lives centers around relationships—relationships marked by depth of understanding and devotion rather than the more casual type that they sometimes experienced when they were young. As David eloquently spoke of his desire for later-life relationships, I was struck by the fact that he was also speaking of genuine, mature freedom, which far exceeds a "do-what-you-please" mentality. He also said, "I want people to remember that I loved them, and I hope I can let the love be genuine, not manipulative, not false or pretentious. I hope I can love and not cling to that which is loved."

Jon also affirms the centrality of love as the meaning of life, both personal life and community life. Love, for him, is not about guilt and a heavy sense of duty, but rather it is about joy and free commitment. Jon spoke of what spiritual growth has meant to him.

> *I have found a wonderful church with a wonderful minister who doesn't get caught up in manmade theology and creeds, but embraces the love of God and the love of family and community. Damn it, that's what it's all about, isn't it?*
>
> *Who is God, and what is the meaning of life? I don't know, although I've thought about it for the last seven years—which have been the freest years of my life. I know I've moved from guilt and duty toward love and freedom and from just acting out the routines set by society toward thinking things out on my own and doing things on my own. I used to wish that when the chronicle of time was written my name might be there, but I don't think it will be. It is enough to love my fellow man and have him love me.*

Another theme that came up as I talked to ESFPs was commitment: "Tell folks to keep engaged with life and whatever it brings to deal with," said one man. "Pay attention to what is happening, for important things lie in the most ordinary things that cross your path. Respond to each person who crosses your path. It really might be an angel in disguise, as they say."

As I talked with Jon and David and the others, I soon became aware that too much "heavy, serious talk," particularly about one's "inner self" or "true self," is likely to call forth humor and some doubt as well, as it did with Jon.

> *I'm not sure I'll ever become my true self. There are too many barriers. I may throw a few bricks off. I do glimpse my true self when I'm having a good time. I'm not hedonistic, but I am sociable. I become alive in sociable circumstances. Yet I strive toward my true self, too. I'm getting closer, and it's not bothering me much that I'm not there. It will evolve. It's not really my crusade.*

CONCLUSION

So, generally, how have these people changed? How are they different in their coming to age period than they were in earlier life? What are the unexpected joys of their later years? I suggest that the gifts of *simultaneous* joy and devotion characterize the later years of the creative Sensing Feeling people. They (particularly the SFJs) find their living is marked more by joy than by obligation and duty. They are increasingly able to embrace their own vision as well as that of those around them, and they care lovingly for themselves and others. They (particularly the EFPs) commit with devotion to that which they love. Some find themselves committed to and lovingly serving Something greater than themselves. They summon energy for personal reflection and sustained, orderly growth. Others feel like they can depend on them and often experience them as people who can relax, enjoy themselves, and delight in life.

CHAPTER 8

REFLECTIONS ON THE GREAT ART OF LIVING

To know how to grow old is the masterwork
of wisdom, and one of the most difficult
chapters in the great art of living.

—Henri Frederic Amiel

*A*s we come to the end of our exploration of creative aging, I will highlight some things that have been said and reflect a bit on what we have learned and why we have undertaken this investigation. As I said previously, I undertook this task because I wanted to know more about the process of creative aging in our time and our culture for myself and for those I care about. I wanted to talk with those who are coming to age creatively, and who know something of the process, in order to use their acquired wisdom, when appropriate, to stimulate our growth.

I believe we will increase our chances for a joyful and creative coming to age period if we prepare for it. Moving through our own adjustments required at midlife and studying the lives of successful people will help. This is not to say, of course, that by preparing we will be denied our own learnings, or that we must all become "wise old people." The people coming to age creatively who share their stories in this book would strongly resist being classified in that way. Our task is not to idealize them, but to select from their generous offerings what is appropriate for ourselves.

I also dare to believe that, by appreciating the gifts of creative aging, we can encourage our youth-oriented culture to modify its attitude. We need to challenge our culture's subtle—and not so subtle—denigration of the process of aging. We need to challenge a belief system that honors productivity, individualism, role playing, and material possessions at the expense of authenticity, true community, and compassion. We must refuse to accept a way of life that overburdens weary midlife people who need a time of renewal and then puts out to pasture those people coming to age who have just discovered their most valuable gifts—or requires them to continue to behave as young people. The best way to challenge culture is to become, as well as we are able, authentic creative people in such numbers that we can require culture to respond.

So what can we say about the creative people who have shared their lives and their learnings with us in this book? They rarely see themselves as giving advice, even as they share their experiences for anyone who wishes to hear. "You just shout down the hall to those who follow you," said one person when asked about advising those who will come after her. "You shout what you know. They may or may not hear, but you've done your part." These people may not have always "gotten everything right"—nor will we. They give us no final solutions, for they would be too glib. "Tell them about our lives, our struggles, and our victories. They'll see we have made it," said one person.

> By appreciating the gifts of creative aging, we can encourage our youth-oriented culture to modify its attitude.

While having changed, these creative people coming to age have also stayed the same. They usually have a sense of self-acceptance—even self-love. They have some ability to contemplate and to act, as well as some ability to deal with complexity and ambiguity. Their lives are marked, at least to some extent, by tolerance, personal responsibility, gratitude, compassion, humility, vitality, and peace. In the chart on page 153 I have summarized some of the qualities common to all people who are creatively coming to age.

Even though much of what these creatively aging people have come to know is similar, often their paths to wisdom have been quite different. Reaching vital contentment may be a process filled with struggle, and may be an unexpected joy of the later years for the searching, self-actualizing Intuitive Feeling person in a way not experienced by the accepting, action-oriented Sensing Thinking person. The later-life joys of connection and relatedness may be filled with struggle for the abstract,

QUALITIES OF CREATIVE PEOPLE
COMING TO AGE

- A deeper, more authentic knowledge of themselves (although this search for self-understanding is more interesting to some than to others).
- A place in relation to others and to their culture (although where that place is will surely vary).
- A connection to Something Greater than themselves (although this may be experienced or conceptualized in very particular, and sometimes idiosyncratic, ways; superficial descriptions of the Something Greater are often rejected or personally reformulated).
- An ability to face some of their own limitations (although their limitations differ widely).
- A sense of fulfillment and integrity in looking back over their lives (although that which brings fulfillment and integrity differs).
- Identifiable changes in behavior and outlook over the years (although some would deny they *tried* to change or grow).

independent Intuitive Thinking person in a way not experienced by the community-loving Sensing Feeling person, who needs to find autonomy apart from community definition.

In the chart on page 45, I identified some of the characteristics common to all people in the three life stages—first half, midlife transition, and second half. In the chart on pages 154–155, I have broken down these stages according to psychological function and have listed characteristics specific to people of each function.

On the basis of my midlife research, interviews with the creative people coming to age in this book, and my own personal and professional experience, I will suggest a few of the most critical messages each of the types might "shout down the halls." As I said earlier, I have no formulas. Throughout this book I have resisted forcing people into categories when the richness of their lives denied this. Inconsistencies and sometimes contradictions have been reported, for they are part of the study of people's lives and of type study as well. I will offer some general comments about each of the sixteen types, selecting and highlighting bits of wisdom people have shared in this book. Listen to the words of people with different type codes. You will hear how they are alike and how they are different as they come to age.

CHARACTERISTICS OF THE
FOUR LIFE STAGES ACCORDING
TO PSYCHOLOGICAL FUNCTION

Intuition and Feeling

First Half of Life	Midlife Transition	Second Half of Life
Accommodation	*Reevaluation*	*Reintegration*
• Caring • Idealistic • Imaginative • Self-actualizing	• Can I be me and not lose you? • Can I dance the music of life with my feet on the ground? • Does this search ever end?	• Hold their own ground and engage others • Accept life and others "as they are" • Make realistic, sometimes limiting choices without stifling the "passion in their veins" • Others feel more accepted and unpressured in their presence

Sensing and Thinking

First Half of Life	Midlife Transition	Second Half of Life
Accommodation	*Reevaluation*	*Reintegration*
• Practical • Realistic • Logical • Productive	• How will I manage if I can't count on my body? • What is this talk of growth and journey about? • Will life be fun again?	• Allow intellectual curiosity and wonder to expand perception • Recognize abundance • Receive with gratitude • Others feel generously welcomed rather than dismissed in their presence

CHARACTERISTICS OF THE
FOUR LIFE STAGES ACCORDING
TO PSYCHOLOGICAL FUNCTION CONTINUED

Intuition and Thinking

First Half of Life	Midlife Transition	Second Half of Life
Accommodation	*Reevaluation*	*Reintegration*
• Visionary • Intellectual • Imaginative • Analytical • Competent	• How can I mentor and serve without "selling out"? • Will I be destroyed if I look vulnerable? • Are there some things and some people I could choose to not redesign?	• Move more freely with less need for protective armor • Attend to the world with detached care and concern • Accept limitations • Others feel more cherished and less judged in their presence

Sensing and Feeling

First Half of Life	Midlife Transition	Second Half of Life
Accommodation	*Reevaluation*	*Reintegration*
• Sensible • Community oriented • Responsive • Caring	• Will I be excluded from the communities that I love? • Will this personal growth process "amount to anything"? • How do I proceed?	• Expand vision and depth • Live with ambiguity • See consequences of action and of inaction • Others feel safe and free in their presence

INFP
FEELING WITH INTUITION

"If it's a good idea, do it."

These passionate, introspective, caring—if sometimes withdrawn—people often speak of the importance of articulating and acting in the face of contradictions and incompleteness. They recognize that time has real limits, is not elastic, and is extraordinarily precious: "I don't have time [now] to fool around. If it's a good idea, *do it*," says one INFP. And they find the vitality to act whether they feel like it or not: "[Now] I can cry over the tragedies in the newspaper every morning, but then I need to get on with my day." They also speak of learning to handle feelings, about being less sensitive, and about love:

> *I can try to put things in perspective [now]. I can talk to myself and say, "If you said something like that it would be to hurt, but not everyone is like you. They may not have intended to hurt you at all." I can choose how to handle my feelings. True respect is about love. It is beyond the golden rule. It requires some letting go of one's own needs in order to love others as they are.*

INFPs who are coming to age talk about doing things their way and accepting their way of doing things—with all its possibilities and limitations: "[Earlier] I got held back by driving others' cars, even though they looked like mine. I do a lot [now]. I'm going to do the best I can, but not sweat and overprepare. My best is all you can ask of me."

They speak about their hunger for life and their passion, and their need to pace themselves. "I don't want to pretend death isn't going to happen. To pretend that cheats us. My greediness for life may come from this realization." And they talk about the contentment that comes with the realization that their culture is not what they wish it was or think it should be, but that they can live with it even as they wish it were otherwise. "Life is as it is, and you make the best of it."

ENFP
INTUITION WITH FEELING

*"I'm on a path and I'm accountable to myself
and to the Creative Force I acknowledge."*

These friendly, enthusiastic, and playful—if sometimes scattered—people often speak about the integrity and the contentment of setting limits. One ENFP expresses these sentiments: "We all have to clip our wings. . . . I started out saying 'I can't' and then learned to say 'I won't' . . . and with 'I won't' came a sense of integrity." And another ENFP says, "If I don't want to spend time with someone, I say, 'Let someone else love that one.'"

They speak of the tension between vitality and contentment. They speak of commitment, discernment, and passion: "I want to tell younger people not to spread themselves too thin, but I also want to tell them to find their passion." They speak of the contentment that comes from getting to know themselves apart from the way others define them. One ENFP says: "I wish someone had told me to be myself. I thought doing God's will was doing what other people wanted." And another feels that "hell is being obligated to be other than oneself."

They speak of learning that they can find contentment with the beauty of the small and ordinary. "We can make beautiful miniatures with the good parts of life that we still have [as we age]." They talk about the contentment that comes with knowing that things work out: "[Things] do work together for good, but not in a Pollyanna way. . . . Zen Buddhists know everything is as it should be, and everything is changing. It is hard to know this when you are young." And they speak of the joy of the senses and of a body that feels good: "It feels good to be in good shape."

INFJ
INTUITION WITH FEELING

"I've learned about feeling and reaching for heights and depths and about not being too afraid. I've also learned not to throw things in people's faces."

These visionary, responsible, and caring—if sometimes self-protective—people often speak of the peace and contentment that come with greater self-acceptance. They speak of the relief that comes when they stop measuring themselves against others: "I've always felt inadequate and surrounded myself with people who, in my mind, were more worthwhile. That's changed."

They speak of pleasure received from intimate contact with others that is free of judgment and blame: "Real contact with my few good friends gives me pleasure. These friends can really talk about things that matter. . . . I don't have to hold back, and I won't be judged." And they talk about the contentment that comes from giving up self-blame as well: "I really don't have regrets about what I did or didn't do. Life is, and it is what it is."

They speak of the vitality that comes from learning not to be afraid. And they speak of the courage, acquired assertiveness, and spontaneity needed to risk placing their true selves in the world, as well as the confidence found in doing so. "I found I could be my true self and I didn't have to give up a damn thing to belong," one INFJ discovered.

They talk of the contentment that comes with accepting "what is" and their ability to preserve some hope and enthusiasm in the face of that: "What happens is, and what is, is okay. I live with it all. . . . Love and service will carry you through." And they speak of tempering intensity and the contentment it can bring. "I have my passion, but I'm no longer caught in the fray," says an INFJ creatively coming to age.

ENFJ
FEELING WITH INTUITION

*"I'm still interested in growing . . . but I've become
a little more choosy about my growing."*

These confident, affirming, and responsible—if sometimes impatient—
people often speak of their struggle between the self-reflection they
desire and the active life they love. "Sometimes it takes a good crisis to get
our attention. We've been so busy in early life moving and shaking that
sometimes we haven't developed much true insight," says one ENFJ.
And, "Bad things have happened to me, but sometimes I wonder if they
were unconsciously set up by me in order to act as hammers. What but
a hammer could get my attention?" says another.

They speak of the relief and contentment they gain from "giving up
responsibility for the universe," or learning the limits of "moving and
shaking." They speak of themselves as less controlling and less compulsive. "I now have, on a scale of zero to ten, somewhere between a zero
and one need to change people," says an ENFJ. "That's a change. I used
to have to save the wounded. It's so refreshing. I say no. I set limits on
rescuing, and it's all within the framework of responsibility."

They speak, sometimes even in spiritual terms, of the danger of living simply to please others. "My guiding prayer now is that I may do
what I was created to do. Pleasing others and being in their community used to be my guiding principle."

They speak of becoming more patient, more content, more dis-
cerning, and more relaxed. "My patience has improved, and I try not to
answer or act too impulsively. I'm more patient with others if I feel they
are neglecting me, or if I can't control their reactions." And, "There was
a time when I would grab anything remotely connected to growth. . . .
I'm now more choosy about my growth experiences."

They speak of the appreciation of the sensory and the immediate.
"The gorgeous azaleas were in their final stages. I stopped and said
good-bye to them."

ISTP
THINKING WITH SENSING

*"There's a difference between whining
and real need."*

These competent, autonomous, and freedom-loving—if sometimes dismissive—people often speak of increasing graciousness and compassion. They frequently speak of "being kinder." They often desire more time with their families and friends. "I've become more tolerant and more sensitive to others' shortcomings," says one ISTP. "I can sometimes say, maybe it wasn't their fault—or if it *was* their fault, then it is really a shame." They speak of being willing to help anyone who needs help, if less willing to help those who can help themselves: "I don't want to be a whiner looking for entitlements. . . . I would be happy, without hesitation, to help an infirm person; but there's a difference between whining and real need."

They speak of spaciousness, of not "blocking out life," and of staying interested in living: "I admire those older folks who don't block out life and who have more to discuss than the weather and what they had for lunch." They talk of the joy of learning: "The reason I did it was it was there to do and I could also learn and experiment."

They talk about an increasing curiosity and interest in reflection. "[Earlier] I would have said, get on with your life. . . . Now I would wonder how all this happened and how it might be handled." They speak of stretching themselves a bit, even though not always enjoying it: "I'm more pliable now." And they speak about commitment and continuity: "Tell [younger folks] about the "monkey principle"—don't let go of one limb until you catch the next one."

ESTJ
THINKING WITH SENSING

"All doesn't depend on me."

These responsible, task-oriented, and hard-working—if sometimes role-bound—people often speak of the increasing importance of relationships. They speak of the value of friendship, especially friendships that are not based on role definition and allow for playfulness and intimacy. A nationally recognized woman felt understanding and joy when upon returning from a lecture tour, her friend asked, "Were you brilliant?"

They speak of the increasing graciousness that comes as they are more able to understand and accept others' viewpoints—even though they may disagree with them. "I'm more patient now when things go wrong and with 'idiots' who can't see things my way," says one ESTJ. "I still get angry with people who espouse injustice, but I've been given insight, and maybe they had different experiences and can't be where I am." Another ESTJ puts it this way: "If your fellow man has let you down, pull him up and maybe he'll see he's not doing exactly right. Kind words go a long way."

They speak of consistency, commitment, and passion. "My commitments haven't changed, but there have been changes in the expression of these commitments," said one person. And they talk about responsibility: "You've got to change structures. To change individuals isn't enough. We're all shaped by the society we live in." But they also speak of the freedom that comes from realizing the limits of responsibility: "What has grown and deepened in my life is the conviction that my call is not to bring an end to every injustice, but simply to serve faithfully."

They speak of gratitude—sometimes even in a spiritual sense—recognizing that they have been the recipients as well as the producers of their lives. "I've made the choices, but God wove the wonderful pattern," says a grateful ESTJ. "I do what I do out of gratitude. I'm so blessed, and I give back because of that."

And they speak of curiosity and openness to wonder: "Dying is going to be a new discovery. I have a lot of curiosity. . . ."

ESTP
SENSING WITH THINKING

"I don't spend much time worrying.
It's not productive."

These active, direct, fun-loving—if sometimes nonempathetic—people often speak of learning to be patient, to wait, and to listen when there is nothing else that can be done: "I don't want to sit around and talk about problems.... I want to do something about them.... [But] I can just listen when that's all you can do. Just listening is often what you can do."

They speak of increasing kindness and regretting their earlier lack of sensitivity to others, particularly to their families. "I wish I had known how they felt, but I didn't think about it," said one ESTP. Or, "Sometimes we say the wrong thing and hurt people, and we have to be big enough to correct it," said another. And they speak of establishing relationships through "helping out." One woman imagined her epitaph to read: "She has done what she could." These people acknowledge regrets, but they do not dwell on them. Life is too short for lingering there.

They speak of learning not to get caught in things they didn't choose and to being committed to the things that they do choose: "We have to be careful not to want every shiny object, every delicious, attractive thing we see—and we see a lot." They speak of being better able to decide where their true commitment lies when they find time to access their own long-term and consistent values. And they graciously call things to which they commit "opportunity" rather than "commitment."

They speak of getting beneath the surface and of not dismissing things that might have been dismissed earlier. One ESTP expressed these sentiments: "There was a time when I would have heard her tragic story and said, I'm sorry, but life is tough. Now I think I would say something like, I wonder how this all happened? This is different."

ISTJ
SENSING WITH THINKING

"When life calls we must risk and live life. . . .
In honestly living, you find life."

These serious, conscientious, task-oriented—if sometimes constricted —people often speak about engaging life and taking risks: "We must risk and live life . . . whatever it brings. In honestly living, you find life." They talk of the need to make changes and the tight, restrictive nature of their earlier lives. One woman expressed the difficulty of this when she said, "I was forty years old before I began to realize that things really could be different." And they speak of trusting the heart: "My future will be the way of the heart. . . . That's enough to know. . . . the rest will follow."

They speak about "being pulled out" of themselves and about opening up and becoming more spacious, which sometimes allows them to receive others without having to label them or place expectations on them. "I don't have to categorize people," says one. "I really can take people as they are, and it has not always been that way." And, "Family was the crucible. Who I am at this moment is because of my experiences with my family," says another.

They speak about graciousness, spaciousness, the limits of judgment, and forgiveness: "Judgment is fallible. You hope you can make the right decisions, but you learn you can live with the wrong ones." And they talk about the importance of personal definition and the connection to their inner lives: "[Earlier life] was dominated by a need to carve out a space. . . . [Now] success isn't what happens outside, but coming to know myself and being happy in spite of external circumstances."

INTP
THINKING WITH INTUITION

*"I feel fortunate to have access to
the next generation."*

These introspective, original, and precise—if sometimes withholding—people often speak of the joy of being able to speak out in a way that can be understood by others and of being able "to make things happen." "At last I want to show up on life's radar," says one INTP.

They speak of the desire to be related to others and to have an impact. They speak of wanting to be of service, which they stress is a word they might not have used earlier. "You really put yourself in service of something. . . . I want to have an impact [on others]," another INTP says. They speak in particular of relatedness and connectedness to young people and of the joy and meaning they derive from teaching them. "I like to teach the young folks to think for themselves, to see beyond the immediate, but to make relationship to the immediate" was the way one INTP expressed this. And, "I'm glad I can speak up when it is appropriate, and I feel fortunate to have access to the next generation," said another.

They speak of coming to know the importance of each particular life, and they do this with tenderness. One woman, who related a story about a woman in the hospital who cried day after day for someone to save her, recognized this in another, and perhaps in herself as well. "She [the hospitalized woman] wanted to be called by name. I knew she thought no one knew her really and she wanted them to know her—to call her by name. She wasn't important to anyone, and that is what she wanted to be saved from."

They speak of self-acceptance and of facing—and accepting—limitations, particularly around relationship difficulties: "I've hurt people, and that's part of my wholeness."

INTJ
INTUITION WITH THINKING

"When there is a bad wind it is good
for my sailing, but bad for my fishing."

These visionary, determined, diligent—if sometimes distant—people speak of connecting with their true selves, a connection that they have often sacrificed to their sense of responsibility: "There used to be one me going on inside and one outside. They're now more the same." And they describe the difficulty they experience when living incongruently: "You can walk sideways, but it tires you out."

They speak of becoming more trusting and more related to others in an intimate way as well, and of being able to lay their armor aside:

> *I wore my armor. . . . There was someone inside it, but you*
> *wouldn't often know it. Armor looks good and protects you from*
> *perceived threats. But now I can sometimes lay my armor down,*
> *at least sometimes with some people.*

These people also talk about self-acceptance: "I've even come to love myself, and that's a change." And they speak of the freedom of lessening blame and judgment—sometimes even in a spiritual sense: "When I stopped beating up on myself, I became less angry with others. I even entertained the idea of a benevolent God, one that didn't want to drive me, demanding more and more, and judge me for my shortcomings."

They also speak of relatedness and connectedness in a spiritual sense to the natural world, to the creative arts, and to dreams. They say peace is triggered by simple things.

> *I went for a long walk under the western sky. . . . I thought if any-*
> *one ever doubted God, I don't see how they could in this situa-*
> *tion. . . . It was the sky that triggered it. It is always something*
> *simple that triggers. It wasn't new information.*

ENTP
INTUITION WITH THINKING

"I spend more time with that [disturbed] woman, who makes heavy demands on my time. Earlier I wouldn't have done that, for I would have seen it as a waste of my time. I'm being kinder to people, you might say."

These expansive, enthusiastic, and curious—if sometimes fragmented —people speak of recognizing the need for focus within the framework of values. "I am beginning to know the difference between important and interesting," said one ENTP. And, "Every newsletter has five million things to do. Too much stuff!" echoed another. "I'm coming to love the pint size as well as the gallon size."

They speak of coming to know the importance of that which is ordinary, common, and often close to home, and they are pleased to learn that they can be practical. "I'm imaginative in a very practical way," reflected one person. They also speak of slowing down and of increasing kindness and compassion: "My edges are softer now. My early years were so full I jumped from one interesting thing to another, but there was little time for reflection—or compassion. . . . I now listen better. I accept more." Another person spoke of patience: "I'm learning to be patient, and I've never been patient. Now, this is how it is and I must live with it."

And they speak of appreciating people they might have previously found uninteresting, if not boring: "I've come to know that it is just as important to be a good person as a stimulating, challenging person. . . . I'm really glad I now know that."

ENTJ
THINKING WITH INTUITION

*"I find a certain selfishness about a
too-personal spirituality."*

These competent, take-charge, responsible—if sometimes imposing—
people speak about the need to break with cultural norms, even as they
continue to see the need to serve culture: "It's very important to break
with the institutional, bureaucratic thing, but I want to make a difference in the world."

They talk about becoming more inclusive and reaching out to those
who are different. "I want to reach out to good, wise people who don't
share my views. . . . That's where my head is now," says one ENTJ. They
speak of the need to slow down and have time for reflection, particularly in order to find their own stand apart from generally accepted
positions and thoughts. "Now when I have time to get my head around
it I can find the position that is mine," explains one person.

They speak of recognizing their weaknesses—particularly around
lack of sensitivity—but they do not dwell on this. "Maybe I should have
done better, maybe I wasn't sensitive enough," says one ENTJ. "I did feel
guilty for a while, but I stopped it." And, "You can't live with someone
more than fifty years and not look stupid sometimes," says another.
"My husband and I can laugh at our stupidities."

They also speak of an increasing capacity to receive and to be appro-
priately vulnerable. They speak of being able to ask for help occasionally:
"I'm even able to ask for a bit of help from others, although that is hard."

ISFJ
SENSING WITH FEELING

*"I have been tutored at the feet of my fears,
and there I have learned courage."*

These solid, hard-working, caring—if sometimes joyless—people often speak of learning to realize the limits of care giving, responsibility, and productivity, even as they continue to care and produce. "When I've done what I can, I say, I've done what I can do; let's don't talk about it anymore," is the way one woman puts it. And, "I want people to understand we have a lot to be thankful for, and I want them to put thankfulness into action," says another. "Elder women are supposed to help younger women. I didn't ask for this role, but it was given to me and I walk in it."

They speak of learning about the flow of work and relaxation, of shared responsibility, and of responsibility "held lightly"—even in a spiritual sense: "After a while, God told me to stand back, that I had done what I could do. I knew it would happen then, so I didn't get in anyone's face for a while." They talk about the need for personal identity and the courage it takes to claim that from the communities they value and wish to please. "I don't have to impress so much," says one person. And "[Now] I am what I am and I've done my thing," says another.

And they speak of making changes when necessary: "Tell young people not to wait as long as I did to pay attention to themselves, and tell them when they discover they're in an unacceptable place, to move on." They also speak of gaining confidence in themselves: "One day I said 'I know,' and it was real. It was really more 'I *know* that I know' and that made all the difference, although I was years in coming to that point."

ESFJ
FEELING WITH SENSING

*"I keep my calendar full, but
I'm not a workaholic."*

These zestful, affirming, and action-oriented—if sometimes nonreflective—people often speak of getting out of role, especially the "happy face" role. "We talk about painful and fearful things; we take the sutures out and look, but we don't think and talk things to death. That would be appalling, for we get together to have some fun," says one ESFJ. And, "It [my book] will have a little sadness, but not too much," says another.

They speak of finding joy, not weariness and heavy obligation, in the service they provide for others: " [Now] I do [what I do] because it makes them happy and it makes me happy too—happy inside." They speak of the joy of humor and the healing of laughter: "Real laughter makes me feel filled with joy." They speak of personal boundary setting and of learning the limits of what can be done: "One day I learned to say 'I won't,' but later I had to learn to say something even harder. I had to learn to say 'I can't.'" And they speak of acceptance: "I've learned you can't change people. I don't try anymore."

ISFP
FEELING WITH SENSING

"I used to say, 'I don't make mountains out
of molehills.'I still don't, but now I also don't
make molehills out of mountains."

These gentle, empathetic, and action-oriented—if sometimes fickle—
people often speak of recognizing their lack of follow-through and of
finding something they can commit to with joy. "I wanted to be a
writer," said one woman, "but I didn't really want to write. I just wanted
to be a writer." And, "Find an interest you don't get tired of," advises
another.

They speak of the struggle between their need for community and
for independence and personal freedom: "You need friends, but you
need freedom, too. I don't want someone underfoot all the time." They
also speak of the benefit of reflection as well as action, often because
they have suffered the consequences of lack of reflection:

> *I used to say, Don't come talk [about a problem]. . . . Come and do*
> *something about it with me. I still like to do things, but I've come*
> *to know that sometimes this attitude can get me into trouble that I*
> *hadn't anticipated. You can't just go along doing things you haven't*
> *thought about because you didn't want to take the time and spend*
> *the energy to understand them.*

They speak about the importance of learning and of curiosity: "I
decided to learn everything I could about the fourteenth century. And,
at eighty-four, I might still decide to learn everything I can about some
important person." They also speak of their increasing willingness to
reflect upon and learn from life: "I used to say, 'I don't make mountains
out of molehills.' I still don't, but now I also don't make molehills out
of mountains."

ESFP
SENSING WITH FEELING

"I think I've become a nicer person in recent
years. Why, in a couple of years, I'm going to
be so nice you won't even know me."

These warm, fun-loving, and humorous—if sometimes easily diverted —people often speak of having to find that to which they can commit with sustained effort. "Tell them to get out of bed in the morning," says one ESFP. And, "Why, I didn't even look when I crossed the street until I had responsibilities," says another.

They speak of learning about the benefits of reflection and of finding what is uniquely theirs to do rather than being caught in unexamined activities. And they speak of the surprise and sadness this can entail: "I feel sad when I realize that although I've always thought I was free, what I was really doing was following others' desires and dodging my right to color outside the lines."

They speak of digging a little more deeply into the events of their lives—of paying close attention not just to the occurrence of the events of everyday life, but also to the importance of such events. "Tell folks to get engaged with life and whatever it brings to deal with," says one person. "Pay attention to what is happening, for important things lie in the most ordinary things that cross your path." And, "I'm social . . . but I do strive toward my true self, too," says another.

They speak of wishing they had planned more carefully: "I wish I had paid more attention to the consequences of my billing and financial requirements in my forties."

And they speak of the desire for and the joy of in-depth conversations and relationships. "I want people to remember that I loved them," says one person. And, "It's enough to love my fellow man and have him love me," says another.

AFTERWORD

I began this book with a personal confession borrowing from the words of May Sarton. I confessed I was writing this book "to find out what I think and to know where I stand" in relation to the process of creative aging. I invited you, the readers to discover what you think and where you stand. Let us now return to the words of Sarton (1992): ". . . the work is more mature than the writer of it, always the message of growth. So perhaps we write toward what we will become from where we are." (p. 208)

Perhaps we write—and read—toward what we will become. May it be so for all of us.

CHARACTERISTICS OF THE SIXTEEN TYPES

$\mathcal{E}$ach type preference (type letter) in one's MBTI code indicates something significant about one's personality structure. This theory proposes two attitudes (Extraversion or Introversion and Judging or Perceiving) and two mental functions (the perceiving function of sensing or intuiting and the judging function of feeling or thinking) for each type category.

Those who prefer the extraverted (E) attitude tend to be energized by their outer worlds, while those who prefer the introverted (I) attitude tend to be energized by their inner worlds. Those who prefer the judging (J) attitude tend to prefer order, closure, and structure, while those who prefer the perceiving (P) attitude tend to prefer spontaneity, open-endedness, and flexibility.

Those who prefer to perceive through their sensing (S) function tend to acquire information through their senses—through what they can see, hear, feel, or in some other way experience—while those who prefer to perceive through their intuiting (N) function tend to acquire information through their imaginations, hunches, and bursts of insight. Those who prefer to make their decisions (their judgments) through their feeling (F) function tend to make choices based on their value systems, while those who prefer to make their decisions (their judgments)

INTROVERTS

ISTJ
Serious, quiet, earn success by concentration and thoroughness. Practical, orderly, matter-of-fact, logical, realistic, and dependable. See to it that everything is well organized. Take responsibility. Make up their own minds as to what should be accomplished and work toward it steadily, regardless of protests or distractions.

ISTP
Cool onlookers—quiet, reserved, observing and analyzing life with detached curiosity and unexpected flashes of original humor. Usually interested in cause and effect, how and why mechanical things work, and in organizing facts using logical principles. Excel at getting to the core of a practical problem and finding the solution.

ISFJ
Quiet, friendly, responsible, and conscientious. Work devotedly to meet their obligations. Lend stability to any project or group. Thorough, painstaking, accurate. Their interests are usually not technical. Can be patient with necessary details. Loyal, considerate, perceptive, concerned with how other people feel.

ISFP
Retiring, quietly friendly, sensitive, kind, modest about their abilities. Shun disagreements, do not force their opinions or values on others. Usually do not care to lead but are often loyal followers. Often relaxed about getting things done because they enjoy the present moment and do not want to spoil it by undue haste or exertion.

EXTRAVERTS

ESTP
Good at on-the-spot problem solving. Like action, enjoy whatever comes along. Tend to like mechanical things and sports, with friends on the side. Adaptable, tolerant, pragmatic; focused on getting results. Dislike long explanations. Are best with real things that can be worked, handled, taken apart, or put together.

ESTJ
Practical, realistic, matter-of-fact, with a natural head for business or mechanics. Not interested in abstract theories; want learning to have direct and immediate application. Like to organize and run activities. Often make good administrators; are decisive, quickly move to implement decisions; take care of routine details.

ESFP
Outgoing, accepting, friendly, enjoy everything and make things more fun for others by their enjoyment. Like action and making things happen. Know what's going on and join in eagerly. Find remembering facts easier than mastering theories. Are best in situations that need sound common sense and practical ability with people.

ESFJ
Warm-hearted, talkative, popular, conscientious, born cooperators, active committee members. Need harmony and may be good at creating it. Always doing something nice for someone. Work best with encouragement and praise. Main interest is in things that directly and visibly affect people's lives.

INTUITIVE TYPES

INTROVERTS

INFJ
Succeed by perseverance, originality, and desire to do whatever is needed or wanted. Put their best efforts into their work. Quietly forceful, conscientious, concerned for others. Respected for their firm principles. Likely to be honored and followed for their clear visions as to how best to serve the common good.

INTJ
Have original minds and great drive for their own ideas and purposes. Have long-range vision and quickly find meaningful patterns in external events. In fields that appeal to them, they have a fine power to organize a job and carry it through. Skeptical, critical, independent, determined, have high standards of competence and performance.

INFP
Quiet observers, idealistic, loyal. Important that outer life be congruent with inner values. Curious, quick to see possibilities, often serve as catalysts to implement ideas. Adaptable, flexible, and accepting unless a value is threatened. Want to understand people and ways of fulfilling human potential. Little concern with possessions or surroundings.

INTP
Quiet and reserved. Especially enjoy theoretical or scientific pursuits. Like solving problems with logic and analysis. Interested mainly in ideas, with little liking for parties or small talk. Tend to have sharply defined interests. Need careers where some strong interest can be used and useful.

EXTRAVERTS

ENFP
Warmly enthusiastic, high-spirited, ingenious, imaginative. Able to do almost anything that interests them. Quick with a solution for any difficulty and ready to help anyone with a problem. Often rely on their ability to improvise instead of preparing in advance. Can usually find compelling reasons for whatever they want.

ENTP
Quick, ingenious, good at many things. Stimulating company, alert and outspoken. May argue for fun on either side of a question. Resourceful in solving new and challenging problems, but may neglect routine assignments. Apt to turn to one new interest after another. Skillful in finding logical reasons for what they want.

ENFJ
Responsive and responsible. Feel real concern for what others think or want, and try to handle things with due regard for the other's feelings. Can present a proposal or lead a group discussion with ease and tact. Sociable, popular, sympathetic. Responsive to praise and criticism. Like to facilitate others and enable people to achieve their potential.

ENTJ
Frank, decisive, leaders in activities. Develop and implement comprehensive systems to solve organizational problems. Good in anything that requires reasoning and intelligent talk, such as public speaking. Are usually well informed and enjoy adding to their fund of knowledge.

From *Introduction to Type®* (5th ed.), by Isabel Briggs Myers. Copyright © 1993 by Consulting Psychologists Press, Inc. Reprinted with permission.

through their thinking (T) function tend to make their choices based on logical analysis.

To have good use of one of each of the pairs of preferences generally allows for successful living. Good development of Extraversion or Introversion, of Sensing or Intuition, of Thinking or Feeling, and of Judging or Perceiving allows one to gather data, evaluate the data, and have some access to both one's inner and outer environments. This development of an adequate four-letter type code is often work for the first half of life.

While any well-developed combination of type preferences can be effective, the type preferences combine in a dynamic way and the combination gives a different flavor to personality. The following descriptions will give you an introduction to the flavor of personality that one may hypothesize from the various combinations of type letters. For a deeper understanding you might read *Gifts Differing* (Myers, 1993) or *Introduction to Type* (Myers, 1993) or consult a qualified MBTI practitioner.

TYPE DEVELOPMENT

$\mathcal{W}$hen we first learn about type we want to understand our preferences (letters) and learn the characteristics of our four-letter type code. (See Appendix A for descriptions of the four-letter type codes.) However, there is much more to type than this. Type theory is dynamic (the preferences interact with each other) and it is developmental. This dynamic and developmental level of type theory is particularly important for midlife and later life, for while we assume that one's essential nature is well described by one's four-letter type code, we also assume that one's essential nature, in its fullness, is not limited to those preferences. Type development hypothesizes that we have some access to the type preferences not in our type codes and that we can expand our personal development by giving some attention to these nonpreferred letters. This expansion beyond a four-letter type code is often the work of later life.

Carl Jung, the theorist behind the development of the MBTI, proposed two mental functions (a perceiving function and a judging function). The preferred perceiving function could be Sensing or Intuition and the preferred judging function could be Thinking or Feeling. Jung also proposed two attitudes (Extraversion and Introversion). Theoretically, although we all use all functions, we have a natural preference for some over others. Our most-preferred mental function is called the *dominant function,* and it is used in our preferred attitude (Extraversion or Introversion). In its support and for its balance, the other preferred mental function not represented by the dominant is called the *auxiliary function* and is used in the opposite attitude of the dominant. For example, if the type code is ENFJ, the dominant is a judging function, Feeling, and it

ISTJ

1 **Dominant** introverted Sensing (S_I)
   Respecting and relying on internally stored data about reality and actual events
2 **Auxiliary** extraverted Thinking (T_E)
   Organizing and structuring the external world with logical systems
3 *Tertiary* Feeling
   Considering the impact of decisions on others
4 Inferior extraverted Intuition (N_E)
   Seeing possibilities and larger connections

ISFJ

1 **Dominant** introverted Sensing (S_I)
   Respecting and relying on internally stored data about people who are important to them
2 **Auxiliary** extraverted Feeling (F_E)
   Organizing and structuring the external world to care for people's daily needs
3 *Tertiary* Thinking
   Assessing logical realities
4 Inferior extraverted Intuition (N_E)
   Recognizing long-term possibilities and connections

ISTP

1 **Dominant** introverted Thinking (T_I)
   Logically organizing vast amounts of specific data about the material world
2 **Auxiliary** extraverted Sensing (S_E)
   Focusing on the immediate material realities in the surrounding world
3 *Tertiary* Intuition
   Seeing patterns in daily events
4 Inferior extraverted Feeling (F_E)
   Factoring in information about people

ISFP

1 **Dominant** introverted Feeling (F_I)
   Living by strong inner values about honoring people and nature
2 **Auxiliary** extraverted Sensing (S_E)
   Focusing on the immediate needs of people in the world around them
3 *Tertiary* Intuition
   Seeing patterns in people's behavior and needs
4 Inferior extraverted Thinking (T_E)
   Using detached logic to evaluate

Abbreviations for Introverted and Extraverted Functions

S_I = introverted Sensing S_E = extraverted Sensing
N_I = introverted Intuition N_E = extraverted Intuition
T_I = introverted Thinking T_E = extraverted Thinking
F_I = introverted Feeling F_E = extraverted Feeling

ESTP

1 **Dominant** extraverted Sensing (S_E)
Delighting in the endless variety of
the world and in spontaneously
interacting with it

2 **Auxiliary** introverted Thinking (T_I)
Using logic and expediency to
solve practical problems

3 *Tertiary* Feeling
Noticing how decisions affect people

4 Inferior introverted Intuition (N_I)
Forming an internal image of the
future

ESFP

1 **Dominant** extraverted Sensing (S_E)
Delighting in the stimulation of
interacting with people and embrac-
ing the variety of sensing experiences

2 **Auxiliary** introverted Feeling (F_I)
Setting priorities by being attuned
to the needs of others

3 *Tertiary* Thinking
Using logic to assess consequences

4 Inferior introverted Intuition (N_I)
Forming insightful internal pictures of people

ESTJ

1 **Dominant** extraverted Thinking (T_E)
Decisively, logically, and efficiently
structuring the external environment to achieve specific goals

2 **Auxiliary** introverted Sensing (S_I)
Internally storing specific, realistic
data about the material world for
quick retrieval

3 *Tertiary* Intuition
Identifying patterns in data; looking at long-term possibilities

4 Inferior introverted Feeling (F_I)
Reviewing decisions in terms of
values

ESFJ

1 **Dominant** extraverted Feeling (F_E)
Acting decisively to create an environment that cares for the practical needs of people around them

2 **Auxiliary** introverted Sensing (S_I)
Internally storing specific, detailed
information about people

3 *Tertiary* Intuition
Developing insights into the
potential of others

4 Inferior introverted Thinking (T_I)
Using detached logic to understand others

Abbreviations for Introverted and Extraverted Functions

S_I = introverted Sensing S_E = extraverted Sensing
N_I = introverted Intuition N_E = extraverted Intuition
T_I = introverted Thinking T_E = extraverted Thinking
F_I = introverted Feeling F_E = extraverted Feeling

INFJ

1 **Dominant** introverted Intuition (N_I)
Becoming centered through insights about people and images of the future
2 **Auxiliary** extraverted Feeling (F_E)
Structuring the external world to support a vision of possibilities for people
3 *Tertiary* Thinking
Taking account of long-range consequences
4 Inferior extraverted Sensing (S_E)
Noticing realistic data about people

INTJ

1 **Dominant** introverted Intuition (N_I)
Relying on clear, complex inner pictures of the present and future as a guide
2 **Auxiliary** extraverted Thinking (T_E)
Using logic to express and implement their ideas
3 *Tertiary* Feeling
Taking account of values
4 Inferior extraverted Sensing (S_E)
Factoring in current reality, details

INFP

1 **Dominant** introverted Feeling (F_I)
Filtering everything through a coherent core of personal values based on honoring individuals
2 **Auxiliary** extraverted Intuition (N_E)
Approaching people and ideas with a sense of curiosity and possibility
3 *Tertiary* Sensing
Focusing on people's daily needs
4 Inferior extraverted Thinking (T_E)
Using detachment and logic to evaluate possibilities

INTP

1 **Dominant** introverted Thinking (T_I)
Logically organizing information into global systems to understand the world
2 **Auxiliary** extraverted Intuition (N_E)
Approaching ideas and information with curiosity; extrapolating patterns into the future
3 *Tertiary* Sensing
Giving weight to external realities
4 Inferior extraverted Feeling (F_E)
Including the perspectives and needs of people

Abbreviations for Introverted and Extraverted Functions

S_I = introverted Sensing S_E = extraverted Sensing
N_I = introverted Intuition N_E = extraverted Intuition
T_I = introverted Thinking T_E = extraverted Thinking
F_I = introverted Feeling F_E = extraverted Feeling

ENFP

1 **Dominant** extraverted Intuition (N_E)
Seeing exciting possibilities for people and enthusiastically pursuing them
2 **Auxiliary** introverted Feeling (F_I)
Evaluating and organizing insights to help people realize their potential
3 *Tertiary* Thinking
Using detachment and logic to analyze options
4 Inferior introverted Sensing (S_I)
Storing and retrieving realistic, practical data

ENTP

1 **Dominant** extraverted Intuition (N_F)
Scanning the environment for options. new and stimulating ideas, exiting possibilities
2 **Auxiliary** introverted Thinking (T_I)
Using logic to critique ideas and plan implementation
3 *Tertiary* Feeling
Factoring in the needs of others
4 Inferior introverted Sensing (S_I)
Considering the limitations imposed by reality

ENFJ

1 **Dominant** extraverted Feeling (F_E)
Providing the structures and encouragement to energize people and groups to grow
2 **Auxiliary** introverted Intuition (N_I)
Developing innovative ways for people and groups to realize their potential
3 *Tertiary* Sensing
Considering immediate, practical options
4 Inferior introverted Thinking (T_I)
Using detached, precise logic to evaluate interactions

ENTJ

1 **Dominant** extraverted Thinking (T_E)
Directing others decisively; structuring the environment to achieve long-range goals
2 **Auxiliary** introverted Intuition (N_I)
Developing strategies, seeing patterns and possibilities in the present and future
3 *Tertiary* Sensing
Including details and the steps necessary to achieve goals
4 Inferior introverted Feeling (F_I)
Assessing the congruity between values and behaviors

Abbreviations for Introverted and Extraverted Functions

S_I = introverted Sensing S_E = extraverted Sensing
N_I = introverted Intuition N_E = extraverted Intuition
T_I = introverted Thinking T_E = extraverted Thinking
F_I = introverted Feeling F_E = extraverted Feeling

From *Introduction to Type® Dynamics and Development*, by Katharine Myers and Linda Kirby. Copyright © 1994 by Consulting Psychologists Press, Inc. Reprinted with permission.

is extraverted. Intuition, the preferred perceiving function, is auxiliary and it is introverted. The *tertiary (third) function* is opposite the auxiliary (its attitude is not agreed upon) and the *inferior function* is opposite the dominant in the opposite attitude of the dominant. Therefore for the ENFJ, the tertiary is Sensing and the inferior is Introverted Thinking. To understand the hierarchy of the dominant, auxiliary, tertiary and inferior functions for each type, you may consult this appendix. For a more thorough explanation of how this hierarchy is established, consult *Introduction to Type Dynamics and Development* (Myers and Kirby, 1994) or consult a qualified MBTI practitioner.

This delicate and complex theory proposes not only a hierarchy of functions, but also their developmental path. Under ideal circumstances the dominant (in its preferred attitude) develops first and is followed by the auxiliary (in its preferred attitude). The tertiary and inferior functions then develop—usually in later life. In later life it is often the tertiary and particularly the inferior function that brings renewal, challenge, and the expansion of personality. It is often, in fact, some development of the tertiary and inferior functions (which are never truly "developed" and which are to be integrated but never substituted for the dominant and auxiliary) that offer the gifts reserved for the later years discussed in this book.

REFERENCES

Corlett, E., and Millner, N. *Navigating Midlife: Using Typology as a Guide*. Palo Alto, CA: Davies-Black, 1993.

Eliot, T. S. *Collected Poems 1909–1962*. Orlando, FL: Harcourt Brace, 1968.

Erikson, E., Erikson, J. M., and Kivnick, H. Q. *Vital Involvement in Old Age: The Experience of Age in Our Time*. New York: Norton, 1986.

Gould, R. "Transformational Tasks of Adulthood." In S. Greenspan and G. Pollock (eds.), *The Course of Life. Psychoanalytical Contributions Toward an Understanding of Personality Development*. Vol. 3: *Adulthood and Aging*. Rockville, MD: U.S. Department of Health and Human Services, 1981.

Guggenbuhl-Craig, A. "Long Live the Old Fool." In *The Old Fool and the Corruption of Myth*. (D. Wilson, trans.). Dallas: Spring Publications, 1991.

Hollis, J. *Tracking the Gods*. Toronto: Inner City Books, 1995.

Jung, C. G. "Stages of Life." In *Collected Works* (R. F. Hull, trans.), Vol. 8: *The Structure and Dynamics of the Psyche*. Princeton, NJ: Princeton University Press, 1981. (Originally published 1960)

Jung, C. G. *Letters*. Vol. 1. (Bollingen Series XCV). Princeton, NJ: Princeton University Press, 1973.

Jung, C. G. *Memories, Dreams, Reflections* (A. Jaffe, ed.). New York: Vintage Books, 1965.

Levinson, D. J., and others. *The Seasons of a Man's Life*. New York: Ballantine, 1978.

Luke, H. *Old Age*. New York: Parabola, 1987.

Maslow, A. H. *Religion, Values, and Peak Experiences*. New York: Viking Press, 1970.

Moore, T. *Care of the Soul*. New York: HarperCollins, 1992.

Morrison, M. C. *Without Night Fall Upon the Spirit*. Pendle Hill Pamphlet 311. Wallingford, PA: Pendle Hill Publications, 1994.

Myers, I. B. *Introduction to Type*. (5th ed.). Palo Alto, CA: Consulting Psychologists Press, 1993.

Myers, K. D., and Kirby, L. K., *Introduction to Type Dynamics and Development.* Palo Alto, CA: Consulting Psychologists Press, 1994.

Nouwen, H., and Gaffney, W. *Aging: The Fulfillment of Life.* New York: Doubleday, 1990.

Oliver, M. "In Blackwater Woods." In *New and Selected Poems.* Boston: Beacon, 1992a.

Oliver, M. "Wild Geese." In *New and Selected Poems.* Boston: Beacon, 1992b.

Palmer, P. *The Active Life: A Spirituality of Work, Creativity, and Caring.* San Francisco: HarperCollins, 1990.

Pearson, C. *Awakening the Heroes Within.* San Francisco: HarperCollins, 1991.

Pretat, J. *Coming to Age: The Croning Years and Late Life Transformation.* Toronto: Inner City Books, 1994.

Rilke, R. M. *Letters to a Young Poet.* (S. Mitchell, trans.). New York: Vintage Books, 1987.

Sarton, M. *Journal of a Solitude.* New York: Norton, 1992.

Sarton, M. "Now I Become Myself." In S. S. Hilsinger and L. Brynes (eds.), *Selected Poems of May Sarton.* New York: Norton, 1978.

Scott-Maxwell, F. *The Measure of My Days.* New York: Penguin, 1968.

Sheehy, G. *New Passages.* New York: Random House. 1995.

Stein, M. *In Midlife: A Jungian Perspective.* Dallas: Spring Publications, 1977.

Steinem, G. *Revolution from Within.* Boston: Little, Brown, 1992.

Teilhard de Chardin, P. *The Divine Milieu.* New York: HarperCollins, 1960.

FOR FURTHER READING

Bianchi, E. C. *Aging as a Spiritual Journey*. New York: Crossroad, 1986.

Brewi, J., and Brennan, A. *Celebrate Midlife*. New York: Crossroad, 1988.

Cole, T., and Winkler, M. (eds.). *The Oxford Book on Aging*. New York: Oxford University Press, 1994.

Friedan, B. *The Fountain of Age*. New York: Simon & Schuster, 1993.

Gould, R. L. *Transformations: Growth and Change in Adult Life*. New York: Simon & Schuster, 1978.

Grant, H., and others. *From Image to Likeness*. Mahwah, NJ: Paulist Press, 1983.

Hollis, J. *The Midlife Passage: From Misery to Meaning*. Toronto: Inner City Books, 1993.

Jacobi, J. *The Way of Individuation*. Orlando, FL: Harcourt Brace, 1967.

Jung, C. G. *Psychological Types* (F. R. C. Hull and H. G. Baynes, trans.), Vol. 6. Princeton, NJ: Princeton University Press, 1990.

Jung, C. G. *The Portable Jung*. (J. Campbell, ed.). New York: Penguin, 1985.

Kroeger, O., and Thuesen, J. *Type Talk*. New York: Dell, 1988.

Levinson, D., with Levinson, J. D. *The Seasons of a Woman's Life*. New York: Knopf, 1996.

Maslow, A. *Toward a Psychology of Being*. New York: Van Nostrand Reinhold, 1968.

Neugarten, B. (ed.). *Middle Age and Aging*. Chicago: University of Chicago Press, 1968.

Miller, W. A. *Make Friends with Your Shadow*. Minneapolis, MN: Augsburg Fortress, 1981.

Myers, I. B. *Gifts Differing*. Palo Alto, CA: Davies-Black, 1993.

O'Collins, G. *The Second Journey*. Mahwah, NJ: Paulist Press, 1978.

Quenk, N. L. *Beside Ourselves: Our Hidden Personality in Everyday Life*. Palo Alto, CA: Davies-Black, 1993.

Spoto, A. *Jung's Typology in Perspective*. Boston: Sigo, 1989.

Terkel, S. *Coming of Age*. New York: The New Press, 1995.

Tournier, P. *Learning to Grow Old*. New York: HarperCollins, 1972.

ABOUT THE AUTHOR

*N*ancy Bost Millner is a Licensed Professional Counselor living and working in Richmond, Virginia. In addition to degrees from Duke University and The University of North Carolina at Greensboro, she holds a Ph.D. degree in counseling psychology from the Union Institute and a Certificate in Spiritual Guidance from The Guild for Spiritual Guidance. Millner has worked for more than thirty years as counselor, university administrator, teacher, consultant, and author in the areas of personal, educational, and vocational development, most recently at Virginia Commonwealth University and The University of Richmond. She has published several articles on type development, the process of midlife, and personal spirituality, and is coauthor of the book *Navigating Midlife* (Consulting Psychologists Press, 1993).

Millner is a founder and past president of the Richmond chapter of the Association for Psychological Type and is a former convenor of Richmond's Jungian Venture Group. Currently she chairs the Chrysalis Group, a nonprofit group designed to support psychological and spiritual growth, and serves as a core faculty member for the Institute for the Enhancement of Dreamwork. When time permits, Millner also conducts workshops, seminars, and retreats in the areas of type development, midlife, creative aging, and personal spirituality.